Presented to

for their participation in the
Glavin Center Global Symposium
on April 7, 2006

M000285718

Global Account Management

Global Account Management
Creating Value

H. David Hennessey

and

Jean-Pierre Jeannet

WILEY

Other Wiley Editorial Offices

John Wiley & Sons Inc., 111 River Street, Hoboken, NJ 07030, USA

Jossey-Bass, 989 Market Street, San Francisco, CA 94103-1741, USA

Wiley-VCH Verlag GmbH, Boschstr. 12, D-69469 Weinheim, Germany

John Wiley & Sons Australia Ltd, 33 Park Road, Milton, Queensland 4064, Australia

John Wiley & Sons (Asia) Pte Ltd, 2 Clementi Loop #02-01, Jin Xing Distripark,
Singapore 129809

John Wiley & Sons Canada Ltd, 22 Worcester Road, Etobicoke, Ontario, Canada M9W 1L1

Wiley also publishes its books in a variety of electronic formats. Some content that appears in print
may not be available in electronic books.

Library of Congress Cataloging-in-Publication Data

Hennessey, Hubert D.
    Global account management / H. David Hennessey and Jean-Pierre Jeannet.
        p. cm.
Includes bibliographical references and index.
    ISBN 0-470-84892-8 (cloth : alk. paper)
    1.   Export marketing.   2.   Export marketing—Case studies.   3.
Marketing—Key accounts.   I. Jeannet, Jean-Pierre. II. Title.
    HF1416.H46 2003
    658.8′48—dc21

                                                            2003007460

British Library Cataloguing in Publication Data

A catalogue record for this book is available from the British Library

ISBN 0-470-84892-8

Typeset in 12/15 pt Garamond by Dobbie Typesetting Ltd., Tavistock, Devon
Printed and bound in Great Britain by TJ International Ltd., Padstow, Cornwall
This book is printed on acid-free paper responsibly manufactured from sustainable forestry
in which at least two trees are planted for each one used for paper production.

Contents

Preface

The impetus for this book came from the companies we serve, who want to serve their global customers better. As we examined the opportunity, it quickly became clear that global account management was very different from traditional sales efforts. While professional sales are important, serving global customers requires a much more complex approach, demanding very serious organizational commitment. In fact, global account management often is a catalyst for major organizational change. To serve a global customer effectively requires a company to assemble cross-functional, cross-business resources focused on serving that customer in multiple geographies, often with a similar product, similar service, and similar price. As open and active executive support is needed for a global account management programme, this focus on global customers will push firms to a global mindset, often changing the way in which a supplier manages its own business.

The underlying premise of this book is that global account management requires a major shift in how we determine customer needs. The traditional method of analysing customer needs is to ask the customer what problems they have and how we can help them. This often extends into supply chain management, where we try to reduce costs through developing a more streamlined supply chain. This traditional approach is necessary but not sufficient to create significant global value.

To really understand a firm's ability to create value for a global customer, we need to understand its industry as well as, or sometimes even better than, the customer does. What is the entire macro business system? What are the key success factors for each set of firms in the system? How is the industry changing? Where are the potential fault lines in the system? What aspects of the industry are currently global? Where is the industry becoming more global? What is your customer's strategy within this industry? What is your customer's source of competitive advantage? How can your firm create significant value that will support your customer's strategy?

The insights gained through this industry-discovery process will allow you to look at your global customer with a new set of global eyes. For example, you would reach nirvana if you achieved insights that allowed you to see that rather than delivering the lowest-priced steel drum to your global petrochemical customer, developing a global drum collection, cleaning and recycling system would create real global value. A new system with standard drum sizes and clear labelling for the customer, to enhance their brand exposure and increase revenue in the marketplace, would create significant value for both your customer and your firm.

We would ask you to examine our approach to global account management with an open mind. Chapter 1 is an introduction and overview of the book. Chapter 2 explains what is driving customers to become global and how they are responding to the global drivers. It also examines the purpose of developing a global account management programme. Chapter 3 is the foundation of the book, how to analyse a global customer's industry. We explore the elements of the business system and how to understand that system. Chapter 4 examines the global logics facing a customer. We explore the global opportunities as well as the local initiatives. Chapter 5 investigates the customer's strategy within its industry. We analyse the strategy's probability of success and highlight opportunities.

Chapter 6 focuses on developing value to support the account strategy. It also examines how we select global accounts and global account managers, as well as how we deliver value to the customer. Chapter 7 focuses on the roles of the global account team, including the global account manager, the executive sponsor and the local account manager. Chapter 8 is concerned with the supporting elements of a global account management system, such as information technology, organizational support, alignment of compensation, pricing and managing the conflicts between global and local interests. The last section of the book includes three case studies on how companies use global account management.

We thank our home institution, Babson College, for supporting us during development of this book. We especially thank the William F. Glavin Center for Global Management at Babson College for funding the initial research on global account management that supports this book.

We also thank the International Management Development Institute (IMD) and Ashridge Management College for providing access to their research facilities and research support staff.

We thank Caleb McCann, Research Associate for W.F. Glavin Center for Global Management, for his dedicated work on the survey of global account executives, as well as development of the global account cases. We also thank Kelly A. Marchetti, Yelena Shayenzon, Celine Charpail, Christine Carr and Marion Power for their help with the collection of materials, typing and creation of exhibits.

This work benefited greatly from the work and experience of numerous executives who face global account management programmes. Our work with DSM, Deloitte Touche Tohmatsu, EuroRSCG and Sun Microsystems has been invaluable in developing our thinking. We would also like to thank the executives who shared their experiences of global account management at IBM, Xerox, Marriott, Steelcase, De La Rue, Fritz, Henkel, Hewlett-Packard, ING, Citibank, Grey Global, Guinness UDV, Maersk Sealand, Reuters and Dun & Bradstreet.

Finally, we thank our families for their support through the drafts and revisions of the book.

We are pleased to dedicate this to Frans Van Helmond, DSM Engineering Plastics, for his dedication to the concept of global account management. It was his constant support in helping us understand how DSM Engineering Plastics could better serve global customers that triggered our interest in this new opportunity.

Additional sources of information on global account management can be found at www.globalaccountmanagement.com.

H. David Hennessey (Hennessey@babson.edu)
Jean-Pierre Jeannet (Jeannet@ids.net)
Wellesley, Massachusetts

Introduction 1

Global accounts are large companies that operate in multiple countries, often on two or more continents, are strategically important to the supplier and have some form of coordinated purchasing across different countries.

Over 20 years ago, professional service firms such as accounting, advertising and consulting recognized that they could accrue multiple benefits from a coordinated global sales and service effort targeted at large companies operating in multiple geographies. For example, accounting firms serving large companies realized that offering a standardized auditing approach to the multiple subsidiaries of a firm located around the world would be beneficial to the corporate parent company, because each audit would follow the same standards in each country. The corporate parent also benefited from having a single accounting firm auditing and certifying its accounts around the world, because this reduced the cost of managing multiple vendors, it could lower the total cost of services and finally, as a large customer the parent company would receive more support and more attention from the global accounting firm.

As shown in Figure 1.1, having a single auditing firm across all countries can be a major benefit. It is not surprising that accounting, advertising and consulting firms were the first to recognize the need to service global customers in a unique way. Large, multi-country companies have attempted to standardize their accounting practices across geographies as well as coordinate their advertising and consulting efforts to leverage the creative and analytical work over many countries, rather than duplicating time, money and effort in every country.

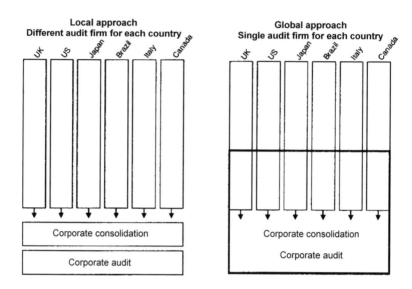

Figure 1.1 Comparison of local versus global audits

At first firms tended to view their effort to serve global customers as a logical extension of traditional national or key account management. National or key accounts are large potential customers operating within a particular country that require additional sales and service resources to serve the customer better. The national or key account manager will often focus on only one or two accounts and develop an account plan to align company resources to serve those national accounts more effectively. Of course, the goal is that by serving these large potential accounts better, the supplier will gain a much larger share of the account's potential business.

A national account management system, where an executive or team is given the responsibility for serving all aspects of a customer's business, is thus a common approach to account management. The national account manager meets regularly with the customer and directs or coordinates activities within the firm to supply that customer. Global account management extends the national account management system across a number of countries to serve important customers that have operations in many countries.

Nevertheless, a study of 21 world-class companies in 1999 reported that almost all the companies felt that global account management was not simply an extension of national account management. The study found that global account management required a unique set of capabilities to be successful. These included strategic thinking, business development, an ability to adapt to different cultures and languages, and the ability to influence internal resources without authority (Weilbaker, 1999). In general, the national account manager was a relationship manager who needed credibility, trust and communication, while a global account manager was more focused on strategic issues and coordination of personnel in different countries.

In the late 1990s, as economic growth began to slow, many firms examined their current customer base and began concentrating more effort on large potential customers. In this process companies in the automobile industry, like Ford, GM, Toyota and BMW; in electronics, like Sony and Philips; in pharmaceuticals, like Merck and GlaxoSmithKline; and in consumer products, like Proctor & Gamble (P&G), Unilever and Kao recognized that they were operating in multiple countries and wanted suppliers who could serve them wherever they operated. For example, General Motors, which had factories in the US, Europe, Asia and Latin America, wanted a resin supplier for car bumpers that could serve all of its locations.

As shown in Table 1.1, we identified a number of significant differences in companies supplying computers, chemicals and food ingredients between the handling of a large customer in one country and serving a global customer. These global companies had decided to serve customers around the world. In many cases this meant having production facilities, research facilities, marketing, finance and accounting efforts dispersed in many countries. Companies realized that they could often better utilize their knowledge and assets through consolidating efforts in certain geographies where unique knowledge or capabilities existed. By developing standard products or standard product platforms, companies could gain economies of scale in R&D and manufacturing. In the same way, they began to

Table 1.1 National/key account versus global account needs

National/key account needs	Global account needs
Relationship building	Global perspective
Leadership	Relationship building
Conflict resolution	Cultural sensitivity and knowledge
Negotiation	Leadership
Boundary spanning	Conflict resolution
Business planning	Negotiation
	Cross-cultural skills
	Boundary spanning
	Business planning
	Industry analytic skills
	Network management skills

explore the benefit of using similar or the same marketing strategies in multiple markets.

As companies have become more global geographically and, more importantly, more global in management, purchasing and strategy, there has been a major growth in new organizational structures to serve them more effectively. The most common organizational approach has been to launch a global account management programme. Companies who have launched such programmes include DHL, Reuters, P&G, Cisco, IBM, Xerox, ABB, Dunn & Bradstreet, Cable and Wireless, Steelcase, Marriott, Citibank, Eastman Chemicals, Hilti, Siemens, Guinness UDV, DSM, Henkel, ING, Maersk Sealand, Hewlett-Packard (HP) and many others. Global account management has been shown to be an effective organizational approach to managing and serving the needs of large global customers. However, it is a difficult and expensive structure to implement and is not successful in all cases for a variety of reasons.

Much has been written about the experience of companies using global account management and this knowledge has been augmented by a number of studies. There is now a set of "key success factors" (KSF) for global account management that is accepted by most experts and practitioners. These KSFs include the global account

Table 1.2 Key success factors for global
account management

Senior executive commitment
Global account selection
Global account planning process
Global account manager selection
Strong IT infrastructure
Alignment of metrics and compensation
Delivery of global values

planning process, the process of selecting global accounts, the process of selecting global account managers, the need for high-level executive support of a global account management system, the need for a global information technology system, and the need for appropriate compensation and metrics. Key success factors for global account management are listed in Table 1.2.

In a recent survey of executives who manage their companies' global account management programmes, we found that these KSFs were acknowledged and supported by leading executive practitioners (Hennessey, 2002). The logic supporting these KSFs was also widely acknowledged by practitioners and researchers. Nevertheless, when looking at the process of creating value through global account management, we found that there were other factors that are not as widely known and practised.

Global account management is an organizational structure designed to serve global customers better. Underlying this objective, the global account management system must create new value for the global accounts. This book examines the KSFs of global account management and focuses on the hidden factors underpinning these KSFs where significant benefits can be realized.

The underlying premise is that to create significant global value, firms must understand their customer's industry and their customer's strategy in that industry, as well as being able to recognize opportunities to create value that supports that customer's strategy.

GLOBAL DRIVERS

To understand global companies, it is useful to understand why they have become global. What internal and external factors have caused firms to move from serving a single market to operating in 50, 100 or 175 countries? What does the global company hope to achieve? How does this company leverage its resources and knowledge in a few countries to enable it to be effective in many countries?

An understanding of these global drivers also illustrates the potential impact of external changes. For example, if the World Trade Organization begins to lose international credibility, what impact might that have on global trade? If China had a financial crisis, how would that affect the automobile industry? Chapter 2, Global Drivers, examines the forces that have pushed firms to become global. It also explores how firms have responded to the global drivers. Finally, it considers why companies have developed global account management to serve their customers.

GLOBAL ACCOUNT PLANNING PROCESS

The global account planning process is acknowledged as a KSF for global account management. It sets clear objectives for the global account and aligns the necessary resources to implement the account plan. Given that the account is global, the account planning process also allows supplier salespeople from around the world to interact and identify additional ways to serve the global account. Often, sales managers in countries where the customer operates are included in the global account planning process, thereby aligning their country plans and goals with the global account plan.

The global account planning process is critical to understanding the global account and determining how to add value. To optimize the process, it is very important that the customer be involved. For example, Maersk Sealand holds an annual global sales meeting that includes the customer in setting goals and action plans for the year.

A weakness of many account plans is that they focus primarily on projects and volume. The supplier focuses on a set of actions in an attempt to get a larger share of potential volume from the account through multiple-level contacts, improved technical service or better customer service. In fact, real value creation comes from understanding the customer's industry, the customer's strategy within the industry and the opportunity for the supplier to contribute to the customer's strategy.

For example, a global coating supplier sold a sophisticated coating used on extruded products. The product needed to be coated as soon as it was extruded to enhance the product's performance. Manufacturing lines were extremely expensive and proprietary. When the coating manufacturer studied the industry in which the extruded product was sold, it determined that this was a high-growth industry and that its customer offered a high-price and high-quality product, but had limited capacity. As the coating manufacturer came to understand the industry better, it realized that speeding up the application of the coating on the extruded product would increase extruding capacity, as well as its customer's profitability. This created a significantly increased value for the customer because the vendor was looking at the customer with a clear industry vision rather than a myopic, customer-only view.

To understand more about the customer's industry and the opportunities to create value that supports the customer's strategy within the industry, we have dedicated three chapters to this process. Chapter 3, Analysing a Global Customer's Industry, provides a set of tools for understanding the industry code, the industry fault lines and a vision for the industry. A comprehensive strategic view of the industry is necessary to understand the arena in which the customer operates. Chapter 4, Analysing the Global Logic of a Customer's Business, focuses on understanding the global dimensions of the customer's industry and the options for better serving global customers. Chapter 5, Understanding the Client's Strategy, utilizes the strategic understanding of the industry and the global logic to understand the global client's strategy. This knowledge allows the supplier to develop a strategy to support the global customer's business.

DEVELOPING AND DELIVERING VALUE

Developing and delivering value to global accounts requires a number of internal steps. Chapter 6 will address these steps, such as determining who should be a global customer and selecting global account managers to develop and deliver value. Global customers with major operations in multiple continents are very important because of their sales volume. These customers will often ask to be treated globally, requesting consistent pricing, terms, products and a single point of contact. However, companies with global account programmes have found that not all global customers translate to meaningful global accounts and that a clear selection process should be developed. Potential global accounts may need to meet a minimum revenue level so that the company can afford the global account management overheads. For example, Marriott International requires that potential global accounts purchase over $25 million annually in hotel services. Companies often want to become a global account so that they can obtain the largest possible volume price discounts. However, global suppliers expect that a global account programme will differentiate them to global customers and therefore result in increased sales volume. While most companies tend to have only 4–15 global accounts, Xerox and IBM have over 100 each. The primary reason that most companies limit the number of global accounts is to maintain clear customer focus.

The critical factor in account selection is to identify accounts where the relationship is strategically important for both parties. For example, one needs to ask whether or not the vendor has over 50 per cent of the customer's sales in its product category and whether the vendor's product is strategically important to the customer. The critical issue is that both vendor and customer must be willing to share business issues and potential product development efforts so that there will be a mutual opportunity to create real value. Although talk about partnership and a strategic relationship may be widespread, a company's lack of willingness to open up may preclude the creation of real value. A good global account must be willing to share its needs and its strategy, as well as to experiment and pilot new ideas.

For example Henkel, a worldwide supplier of adhesives, uses a set of hard and soft factors to select its ten global accounts. The hard factors are total purchases from Henkel, profitability and market share. The soft factors are being market driven, innovation driven and cooperation minded. Every firm uses some hard factors like size, potential growth and number of countries, but the soft factors like leader in its field, being innovation minded and having a willingness to share strategic plans are often the deciding factors.

As another example, BMW wanted to create vehicle owner's manuals that were personalized and less expensive to produce. Most vehicle owner's manuals included material and instructions for all possible options in at least four different languages. The traditional owner's manual was about an inch and a half thick. This practice wasted paper, led to high printing costs and had high associated storage costs. Xerox worked with BMW for almost a year to create a personalized print-on-demand owner's manual. With this solution, BMW was able to provide an owner's manual that was personalized, with the buyer's name printed on the front, in the buyer's preferred language, and with instructions that addressed only the specific options purchased. The new owner's manuals are 80 per cent thinner than those previously used and are printed on demand, thus eliminating storage and shipping costs. This solution was only possible because BMW was open to innovation and willing to experiment (Hennessey, 2002).

Selecting global account managers

A successful global account management programme requires high-quality global account managers. Therefore, it is not surprising that companies report the selection of global account managers to be one of the KSFs for effective global account management. Global account managers need to be able to build significant working relationships with CEOs, COOs and senior executives. They also need to be perceived as respected senior managers in their own organization in order to coordinate and direct the activities of others who may not be under their direct authority. As global account managers interact with individuals from both the customer and supplier organizations, from multiple cultures, it is expected that they should be capable of building and maintaining trusted relationships across diverging cultures, geographies and economies.

A common misstep in selecting global account managers is the assumption that all good national or key account managers can be good global account managers. This may not be the case. Many national account managers do not have the cross-cultural skills and the broader business acumen required to be successful global account managers.

Critical skills needed by global account managers are the ability to analyse an industry, understand competitive strategies and identify scenarios where a supplier can contribute to a customer's strategy. They are more closely aligned with the skills of a general manager than those of a senior salesperson. Many companies with global account management programmes find a need to provide additional training in areas where global account managers may be deficient.

For example, in 2000 Xerox elevated a telecommunications equipment manufacturer from a national account in the United States to a global account because of its global expansion. In this case, the person who held the position of national account manager did not become a global account manager because Xerox industry management did not feel that the person was sufficiently capable of taking on the additional responsibility. National account managers and global account managers have similar jobs at Xerox, except for the degree of complexity, difficulty and cultural acumen required. A national account manager with less refined human management skills might perform well in the US because he or she is dealing primarily with other Americans and does not have to master other languages or deal with cultural difficulties (Hennessey, 2002).

Value delivery

Developing and delivering value require unique skills. In addition to understanding the customer's industry (Chapter 3), the global logic of the industry (Chapter 4) and the customer's strategy (Chapter 5), a global supplier must develop a culture to support global account management and therefore the global customer. A company with such a culture will understand the problems the global account faces as well as how the customer's needs may be changing. The delivery of global value to a customer requires ongoing communications, supported by a developed relationship. Chapter 6, Developing and Delivering the Value Proposition, explains the skills and competencies needed within the supplier organization to successfully implement and maintain superior value delivery. It includes the selection of global accounts and global account managers. The chapter also discusses the development of a strong global account management culture and delivering the value proposition.

THE GLOBAL ACCOUNT MANAGEMENT TEAM

It is impossible for a global account manager individually to serve a global account. The effort is usually handled through a team of people, including the executive sponsor, the global account manager, account managers from the relevant countries and key service managers. Chapter 7, The Global Account Management Team, explains the development of the team, the role of senior management and the process of managing the account relationship.

Senior management commitment

A global account management programme needs senior management commitment for three reasons. First, global customers expect to meet with senior managers from their key supplier on a regular basis.

Second, allocating essential people and resources to global account management often results in key people and resources being moved from particular countries and regions to serve the global account better. Third, senior managers are often involved in making trade-off decisions between local business units, global business units and global accounts. Senior management needs a commitment to the long-run benefits of a global account to make the necessary trade-off decisions appropriately.

Senior management commitment adds the most value by its indirect support of the global account manager. The global account manager can be one person or a team, often located in the country where the customer is headquartered. For the global account manager to create value for the global account, this executive must coordinate activities across geographic and business unit boundaries. The ability to accomplish these tasks is a direct reflection of senior management commitment. Without this commitment, the global account manager will not have sufficient clout to coordinate and direct activities and influence priorities across traditional divisional and geographic organizational structures.

For example, senior management was responsible for the success of Reuters' global account management programme. All team members involved in the programme reported directly to a senior vice-president. And at Xerox, at the end of each quarter, lead sales representatives may have the opportunity to sell a few additional units at a discounted price to a global account to benefit their local P&L statement, which would disrupt the global account management strategy. Therefore, even though they may have the opportunity to lower prices at a global account, they would resist the temptation rather than risk upsetting senior management at Xerox (Hennessey, 2002).

The ability of the global account management team to operate is a function of its ability to balance the global and local needs of the customer. In addition, much of the global account strategy will be implemented through local sales and service staff, so the global account team must manage these transactions as well.

SUPPORTING AND IMPLEMENTING GLOBAL ACCOUNT MANAGEMENT

The process of supporting and implementing a global account management programme requires a number of important elements, which Chapter 8 addresses. First, an information technology infrastructure is required to help the company understand and manage the interaction with the customer. Second, the measures, metrics and rewards need to be aligned; and third, pricing and contracts must be addressed.

Information technology infrastructure

Global account management requires a sophisticated infrastructure of information technology, measurement and rewards, and communications to support the development and implementation of a global account management programme. A key success factor for global account management is a robust information technology system that may include a global customer relationship management (CRM) system. A sophisticated global IT system will track the progress of a global account in terms of orders, back orders, shipments, accounts payable, complaints, returns etc. The people serving the global account need this information to manage the account. They also need a sophisticated system so that they can record what is happening within different divisions of the global account, thereby enabling them to communicate more effectively with each other. At DSM Engineering Plastics, global customers often commented that the DSM global account manager knew more about what was happening at the customer's company than within the company's own global purchasing department.

However, the real importance of a robust IT system is the way it creates value for the customer. For example at Marriott International, which serves IBM, the global account manager was able to track IBM's conference cancellations globally. These were costing IBM over $2 million annually. Through their global account management programme, Marriott International's account managers created an internal electronic bulletin board for IBM employees to purchase cancelled space, thereby reducing cancellation fees and substantially reducing IBM's costs. Nevertheless, a robust IT system creates real value only when the global account team can take a global view of the customer and identify potential value-creation opportunities (Richard & Wilson, 2000).

Measurement, metrics and rewards

The sales function has always included some form of measurement, metrics and rewards tied to sales, profit or market share. Therefore, it is not surprising that measurement, metrics and rewards form a KSF for global account management. Marriott International, Xerox, Steelcase and IBM all have measurement systems to track the sales of their global accounts and the implied results of the global account management effort. Of course, this may cause some tension between the global account manager and the regional or local manager, unless the vendor has some form of double counting that gives full credit for the sale to both the local and global units. A number of suppliers also track market share, completion of identified projects and customer satisfaction.

All these metrics attempt to measure the success of the vendor with the global customer. However, the underlying success of any global account management system is the impact it has on the customer's overall strategy and profitability. Real value is measured only through understanding the customer's industry, the customer's strategy and the supplier's role in supporting that strategy.

Citibank's global account management programme uses a shadow P&L system. A specific global customer is identified with every transaction. The system gives Citibank the ability to look at revenues and, using product costs, establish the contribution associated with those revenues for every single customer, giving it a total market view (Hennessey, 2002).

CONCLUSION

Global account management is a new organizational form designed to serve global customers better. While there are some similarities with national and key account management programmes, the real value comes from understanding the customer from a global perspective.

For example, when DSM Engineering Plastics found that its largest customer was losing share to lower-quality Chinese manufactured parts, it brought its understanding of how the industry was changing to bear in solving the problem. Within a year both DSM and the customer had built facilities in China. DSM has also developed a specific colour additive, which could not be replicated by other manufacturers, thereby reducing the threat of lower-quality copied products.

Global account management often adds a layer of organizational structure to facilitate the management of the company's resources to serve a select set of global accounts. To afford this additional expense, the system must be driven by the mantra of identifying new value-creation opportunities. These opportunities are beyond the traditional supply chain rationalizations and global price discounts. Value comes from an expert knowledge of the customer's industry, the KSFs in that industry, an understanding of possible industry fault lines and the strategy of the customer to win in that industry. When vendors can identify and create value that supports a customer's strategy, the global account management programme is more likely to be successful.

The combination of our research, discussions with executives who have launched and managed global account management programmes and hundreds of articles and presentations on global account management has led us to redesign the process of managing global accounts. The process of identifying and delivering value for the global account is summarized in Figure 1.2, which also provides an overview of the book.

In the past, the general approach for global account management was to use the key or national account management approach with

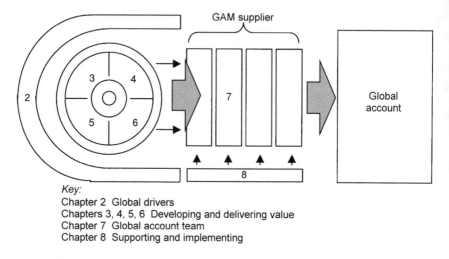

Key:
Chapter 2 Global drivers
Chapters 3, 4, 5, 6 Developing and delivering value
Chapter 7 Global account team
Chapter 8 Supporting and implementing

Figure 1.2 Overview of the global account management process

the addition of multiple geographies. This can provide results, but falls short of generating the breakthrough innovations that lead to a strong global buyer–supplier partnership. Discovering the real hidden opportunities that global account management can create begins with understanding the environment in which the global account is operating and the forces that are causing the customer to think and act globally, which are covered in Chapter 2. Next it is critical to develop an in-depth understanding of the customer's global industry. Where is the industry today? Where is the industry going? Where are the potential fault lines? This in-depth analysis leads to an understanding of the industry and the key success factors within it. These are discussed in Chapter 3.

Customers develop global strategies based on the structure of the industry and its global aspects. The global aspects of an industry could be the customers, their needs, the competition, economies of scale and so on. Chapter 4 examines the global logic of the customer's industry, an understanding of which is needed to grasp the various strategic options within the industry.

The success or failure of a global company depends largely on its strategy within its industry. What is its strategy? How does the global customer leverage its assets? What is the customer's source of competitive advantage? What firms are winning and losing in this industry and why? The process of analysing the global customer strategy within an industry is discussed in Chapter 5. This analysis of the global customer allows a supplier to look through the eyes of an industry expert who understands what is needed for a winning strategy. Only after this analysis is done is it appropriate to begin developing the global account plan.

For example, a foam producer supplied foam to a car seat manufacturer for years based primarily on providing the lowest cost per square metre of foam. The foam manufacturer continually tried to develop differentiated foam with unique attributes, but was unsuccessful. At one point, the foam manufacturer developed a process to produce foam that was half an inch thinner, but with the same cushioning benefit and a slightly higher price. However, the seat manufacturer rejected this thin foam. Then the foam manufacturer decided to analyse the global auto industry and identified winning strategies. Automotive companies had designed cars to be lighter and more aerodynamically efficient to reduce fuel consumption. This had resulted in the cars' exterior looking more and more alike. The auto manufacturers shifted resources to the cars' interior, which became a major point of differentiation as they attempted to boost comfort, improve acoustics and add new features to lure new customers. Under this new view of the industry the foam manufacturer uncovered a major benefit of the thin foam. It provided the same comfort but with greater headroom, a very attractive benefit for the car manufacturing marketing department that was not appreciated by the seat manufacturer. With this new industry understanding the foam manufacturer improved the seat manufacturer's strategy by offering a differentiated seat to its automotive customers, a winning combination for both companies. The process of contributing to the global customer's strategy will be discussed in Chapter 5.

As illustrated in the thin foam example, contributing to a global customer's strategy can be a powerful tool. Ultimately, global customers will select their global suppliers based on their perception of the value created by the supplier at a competitive price. A major element of a global account plan is a clear understanding of the value proposition that the global customer will be offered. A change in end-user needs, not meeting those needs or having a unique way to combine products and services are all potential sources of a value proposition. A major component of the global account plan will be the development and delivery of the value proposition to the global customer. This will include aligning the supplier's resources to deliver a superior value proposition, which will be discussed in Chapter 6.

Global account management is a complex process involving hundreds of people in both the customer's and supplier's organization. These people are located around the world in different time zones, with different cultures and priorities. The global account management team described in Chapter 7 will help orchestrate the delivery of value to the global customer.

A number of key elements support the global account management process, such as the information technology infrastructure, metrics, pricing and contracts, all of which are discussed in Chapter 8. Finally, to give an example of global account management in action, we have included case studies from Xerox, Marriott and Hewlett-Packard.

Global Drivers

What is driving customers to think and operate globally? How do customers respond to these drivers? It is important to understand these issues, as they drive the demand for global account management. The factors shown in Figure 2.1 also provide an insight into the needs of global customers, the changes in industry structure and the logic behind a customer's global strategy. As we examine the factors that drive firms to become global, it is helpful to think about how these forces influence industry structure, competitive positioning and global strategy.

MACROECONOMIC FACTORS

Growth in world trade

World trade has grown sixteenfold since 1950, far surpassing the growth in world total gross national product (GNP). The opening up of world markets has fuelled this growth. In 1944 the Bretton Woods conference of world leaders led to the establishment of the General Agreement on Tariffs and Trade (GATT). The original group of 23 countries agreed to work together to reduce barriers to free trade, the largest being protectionism. Protectionist legislation tends to be in the form of tariffs, quotas and/or qualitative trade restrictions. Protectionism slows the import of goods and services into a country. GATT, which was superseded by the World Trade Organization in 2000, now includes 144 member countries with another 31 countries waiting to join. Its main advantage is that it has reduced tariffs from 40 per cent in 1947 to an estimated 4 per cent in 2000.

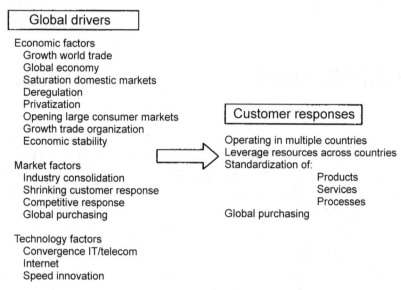

Figure 2.1 Summary of global drivers and customers' responses

The opening of world markets has given companies an opportunity to expand by either exporting to other countries or making direct investments in multiple countries to serve local market needs. The growth in international trade has caused the national economies of the world to become much more closely linked and interdependent because of their imports, exports and foreign direct investments. As companies have surveyed the opportunities, they have focused on larger markets, markets with above-average growth, markets with favorable cost structures and markets that are best located to serve multiple countries.

When assessing where to locate sales, marketing, R&D, manufacturing and management resources, companies have begun to view the world as a chessboard, as shown in Figure 2.2. The squares on the chessboard represent different countries: some are must-win squares, others are nice to have, others may be less important. The pieces on the board also have different values: the sales effort may be best represented by pawns, which need to provide the front line. The knights are strategically placed, representing manufacturing. The king and queen represent power, to be used to capture must-win markets.

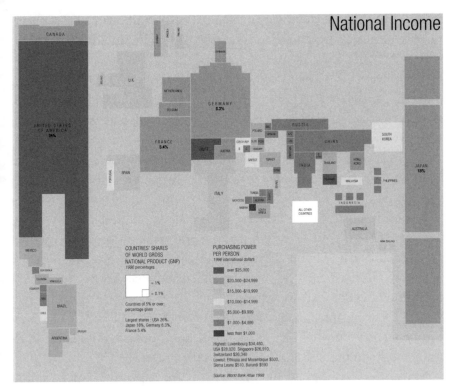

Figure 2.2 The global chessboard. Reprinted with permission from Dan Smith, *The State of the World Atlas*, 6th edition. Copyright ©Myriad Editions Limited

The reduction in barriers to cross-border trade has opened up the global chessboard to many more companies.

The global economy

The global economy is in a state of transition from a set of strong national economies to a set of interlinked trading groups. This transition has accelerated over the past few years with the fall of the Berlin Wall, the collapse of communism, and the coalescing of the European trading nations into a single market. The investment by Europeans, Japanese and Americans in one another's economies is unprecedented. US companies create and sell over $80 billion per year in goods and services to Japan. Foreign direct investment of private funds peaked in

1998 at $180 billion, and was estimated to be $140 billion in 2002. China is one of the largest beneficiaries, receiving $50 billion in 2002 (Donnelly, 2002). As companies globalize, manufacturing becomes more flexible and engineers have instant access to the latest technology. For instance, microchips designed in California are sent to Scotland to be fabricated, shipped to the Far East to be tested and assembled, and returned to the United States to be sold.

There is no doubt that the world is moving towards a single global economy. Of course there are major difficulties on the horizon, such as the development of a market-based economy in eastern Europe, a reduction in hostilities and the establishment of political stability in the Middle East and parts of eastern Europe, and stabilization and growth in the former Soviet Union. However, anyone serving global customers needs to understand the interdependencies that form the world economy in order to comprehend how a drop in the US discount rate would affect business in Stockholm. Another example would be how Britain's entry into the European Monetary System would affect both foreign sales in the UK and UK sales to the rest of the EU.

Since the economies of the world are becoming increasingly interlinked, small changes in markets are felt in many places around the world. For example, in June 1999 the world equity markets rose in Europe, China and Tokyo as traders around the world anticipated that US Federal Reserve chairman Alan Greenspan would raise interest rates on June 30 by 0.25 per cent. Information technology, telecommunications and the Internet have made information on worldwide prices, products and profits available globally and instantaneously. With markets thus more transparent, buyers, sellers and investors can learn about the best opportunities, lowering costs and ensuring that resources are used most efficiently.

These changes are fundamentally altering national, regional and global economic systems. As the speed of change accelerates, successful companies will be able to anticipate the trends and either take advantage of them or respond to them quickly. Other companies will merely watch the changes going on around them and wake up one day to a different global marketplace with new rules.

Saturation of traditional markets

As the local economies of the developed countries of Europe, North America and Japan have become fully developed, there has been a tendency for population growth to decline and the domestic market in these countries to become saturated. This leads many companies to consider growth alternatives in other markets. Initially the developed countries began selling products to each other. For example, cheeses, wine and perfume manufactured in France were marketed in the US and Japan as well as other European countries. US automotive manufacturers moved to Europe, while the Japanese auto manufacturers moved first to the US and then to Europe.

As market opportunities decreased in the developed countries, manufacturers began to look for new markets in the developing countries. The saturation of domestic markets encouraged companies not only to explore exporting, but also to make direct investments in these new markets, including building factories, making acquisitions of firms in other countries and forming alliances. As companies invested in non-domestic markets, an increasing percentage of revenue came from other countries, followed by the development of managers with multi-country experience. These managers became the global visionaries who helped move the pieces on the global chessboard.

Deregulation

A further trend affecting global markets is the rapid deregulation of business everywhere. The United States is generally considered to have taken the lead with its deregulation of several industries, particularly transportation, airlines, banking and telecommunications. The general concepts of deregulation were readily absorbed by some other governments, the United Kingdom among them. As part of the European integration drive, deregulation also became an important issue in Europe.

For example, the European Union has opened its telecommunications market. The long-standing monopolies of the national telephone companies in most European countries are giving way to more open competition along the US and UK models. Although data communication has already been deregulated, the trend now is to include regular voice communications as well. Deregulation will bring more competition because the local phone companies can no longer count on their monopolies. It will also create opportunities for other carriers, such as AT&T from the United States and the various regional operating companies, to expand overseas. In mobile communications these US firms have expanded into other markets, usually linking with local partners. NTT DoCoMo, a Japanese mobile communications firm, has entered the US through a partnership with AT&T Wireless.

Similar efforts are underway in Asia, where telecommunications markets are growing rapidly. AT&T and British Telecom have taken 30 per cent ownership of Japan Telecom, the third largest player in Japan. Other efforts have occurred in Japanese financial markets, where substantial deregulation is under way in banking and insurance. This is important to international banks, particularly with respect to financial derivatives.

Deregulation is typically accompanied by liberalization and the opening of markets to foreign competitors. This trend therefore adds to the set of opportunities available for firms to expand internationally.

Privatization

Another trend affecting global markets is the rush towards privatization. Under privatization, countries sell government-owned agencies, organizations and companies to private stockholders or other acquiring firms. Starting in the late 1970s and early 1980s, acts of privatization overtook nationalization, and for the period 1990–1992 the United Nations counted more than 150 privatizations (United Nations, 1993). Some of the earliest examples of privatization came from the United Kingdom, where the government privatized airlines (British Airways), telecommunications companies (British Telecom) and many utilities (e.g. British Airports Authority).

Privatization has swept through over 100 countries, which have privatized 75 000 state-owned companies. The results have been good in central and eastern Europe as well as the Baltic states. They have been poor in Russia, Armenia, Georgia, Kazakhstan, Moldova, Mongolia and Ukraine. The drive towards privatization was particularly strong in Poland, the Czech Republic and Hungary. Philip Morris, a US-based food and tobacco company, was able to acquire a stake in the Czech Republic's Tabak, a company with a tobacco monopoly. The Czech government indicated that the monopoly would eventually end; however, Philip Morris expected to get a head start through its acquisition. Many privatizations in Poland and the Czech Republic occurred through the distribution of shares, or coupons, to the local population. Nevertheless, the effort to privatize state industry in many parts of eastern Europe has resulted in significant opportunities for foreign firms to acquire the privatized companies.

The trend towards privatization is expected to continue, with approximately 1300 separate deals anticipated worldwide, not including any activity in eastern Europe. Whenever privatization occurs, it is typically related to decreasing involvement of the local government in that particular industry or sector. This change invariably leads to further trade liberalization and deregulation. Both phenomena generate increased opportunities for global companies.

Opening up of large consumer markets

There are large market opportunities in eastern Europe, Asia and Latin America, fostered by such events as the fall of the USSR in the 1990s along with the opening up of India and China. As shown in Table 2.1, 57 per cent of the world's population is in Asia, with the countries of India and China (37.5 per cent of world population) offering a large growth potential as these economies develop and the purchasing power of consumers increases. Through alliances, joint ventures and acquisitions many firms have entered these markets.

Table 2.1 Regions' share of world population

Region	%
Asia	57
Africa	13
Europe	13
Latin America	8.5
North America	5
Near East	3
Ocean	0.5

Source: *State of the World Atlas*, 6th edition, 1999, p. 15.

In addition to being a large market opportunity, many of these new markets also have lower labour costs, therefore giving firms an opportunity to begin manufacturing in these countries and exporting to other markets with higher labour costs. For example, Electrolux purchased Lehel Company in Hungary in 1991, which quickly started exporting small freezers to the rest of Europe.

Growth of trade organizations

In addition to the World Trade Organization, a number of countries have entered into market agreements with their neighbours to reduce or eliminate all trade barriers. Table 2.2 shows a summary of the major market agreements supporting free trade.

For example the European Union, which includes 15 countries and has agreed to add 10 additional countries by 2004, has reduced trade barriers that inhibit the free flow of products, services, people and money. The launch of the European Monetary Union resulted in a single currency, the Euro, for the 11 countries that have agreed to participate in the Union.

The North American Free Trade Agreement, which includes Canada, Mexico and the United States, has reduced trade barriers between these countries. Mercosur, the Indian Common Market and

Table 2.2 Summary of market agreements

European agreements

EUROPEAN ECONOMIC AREA		*EUROPEAN UNION*	
Austria	Italy	Austria	Italy
Belgium	Liechtenstein	Belgium	Luxembourg
Denmark	Luxembourg	Denmark	Netherlands
Finland	Netherlands	Finland	Portugal
France	Norway	France	Spain
Germany	Portugal	Germany	Sweden
Greece	Spain	Greece	United Kingdom
Iceland	Sweden	Ireland	
Ireland	United Kingdom		

EUROPEAN MONETARY UNION		*EUROPEAN FREE TRADE ASSOCIATION*	
Austria	Ireland	Austria	Norway
Belgium	Italy	Finland	Sweden
Finland	Luxembourg	Iceland	Switzerland
France	Portugal	Liechtenstein	
Germany	Spain		
	The Netherlands		

African agreements

EAST AFRICA COOPERATION		*ARAB MAGHREB UNION*	
Ethiopia	Tanzania	Algeria	Morocco
Kenya	Uganda	Libya	Tunisia
Sudan	Zambia	Mauritania	

FRENCH AFRICAN COMMUNITY		*ECONOMIC COMMUNITY OF WEST AFRICAN STATES*	
Benin	Equatorial Guinea	Benin	Liberia
Burkina Faso	Gabon	Burkina Faso	Mali
Cameroon	Guinea-Bissau	Cape Verde	Mauritania
Central African Republic	Mali	Gambia	Niger
Chad	Niger	Ghana	Nigeria
Congo	Senegal	Guinea	Senegal
Ivory Coast	Togo	Guinea-Bissau	Sierra Leone
		Ivory Coast	Togo

(*continued*)

Table 2.2 (*continued*)

American agreements

MERCOSUR (SOUTHERN COMMON MARKET)	
Argentina	Paraguay
Brazil	Uruguay

ANDEAN COMMON MARKET (ANCOM)	
Bolivia	Peru
Colombia	Venezuela
Ecuador	

CENTRAL AMERICAN INTEGRATION SYSTEM	
Costa Rica	Honduras
El Salvador	Nicaragua
Guatemala	Panama

CARIBBEAN COMMUNITY AND COMMON MARKET	
Antigua and	Jamaica
Barbuda	Montserrat
Bahamas	Saint Kitts-Nevis
Barbados	Saint Lucia
Belize	Saint Vincent
Dominica	and the Grenadines
Grenada	Suriname
Guyana	Trinidad and Tobago
Haiti	

US–CANADA FREE TRADE AGREEMENT	
Canada	United States

NORTH AMERICAN FREE TRADE AGREEMENT	
Canada	United States
Mexico	

Asian agreements

ARAB COMMON MARKET (ACM)	
Egypt	Syria
Iraq	Kuwait
Jordan	

ECONOMIC COOPERATION ORGANIZATION (ECO)	
Afghanistan	Pakistan
Azerbaijan	Tajikistan
Iran	Turkey
Kazakhstan	Turkmenistan
Kyrgyzstan	Uzbekistan

ASSOCIATION OF SOUTH EAST ASIAN NATIONS (ASEAN)	
Brunei	Myanmar
Cambodia	Singapore
Indonesia	Philippines
Laos	Thailand
Malaysia	Vietnam

ASIA PACIFIC ECONOMIC COOPERATIVE (APEC)	
Australia	New Zealand
Brunei	Papua New Guinea
Canada	Philippines
Chile	Singapore
China	South Korea
Hong Kong	Taiwan
Indonesia	Thailand
Japan	United States
Malaysia	Vietnam

the Central American Integration System operate in Latin America and have all agreed to negotiate to form the Free Trade Area of the Americas (FTAA), which would include NAFTA by 2005. All of these trade organizations have agreed to the reduction of tariffs and have a goal of increasing trade between the member countries. More trade means that it is easier for companies to expand into these neighbouring countries with few or no restrictions.

Economic stability

Stability in the international economy is a prerequisite for world trade. The International Monetary Fund, the World Bank and the Group of 7 all help support international stability in world markets.

The International Monetary Fund's main goal is to promote orderly and stable foreign exchange markets, maintain free convertibility among currencies, reduce impediments to trade and provide liquidity to counteract temporary imbalances in international payments. The IMF has loaned money to Thailand, Brazil, South Korea and Argentina to help stabilize these countries' economies when in financial difficulty.

The World Bank provides long-term loans to developing countries, often to help improve their infrastructure in terms of roads, electricity and water projects.

The Group of 7 – consisting of finance ministers and central bank governors from Britain, Canada, France, Germany, Italy, Japan and the United States – meets regularly to discuss the world economy. Its members work informally to stabilize the world economy and reduce extreme disruptions.

The collective work of these agencies helps reduce the severe disruption of a single country's economy that would flow over into the world economy. This economic stability reduces the risk of direct foreign investment into many countries as well as improving the market for imports and exports.

MARKET FACTORS

Consolidation of industries

Certain industries have very high fixed costs. For example, the cost to build a new semiconductor chip manufacturing plant can rise to $2–4 billion, while building a new automobile plant could cost $5–10 billion. As the amount of fixed costs in these industries increased companies found it necessary to become larger, often by acquisition, to get a sufficient return on their fixed investment. This drive for economies of scale has affected the industries for automobiles, airplanes, pharmaceuticals, semiconductors, large appliances and many others.

By definition, these consolidated industries with a few large players must operate in most of the world's markets, such as the US, Europe, Japan, China, Brazil and Russia. For example, most of the world's automobile manufacturers have operations in China and Brazil.

Shrinking customer base

The consolidation of a number of industries, including electronics, automobile, aircraft, accounting and pharmaceuticals, has resulted in a smaller number of larger customers. These big customers represent a large portion of the potential market for many suppliers. This has resulted in a significant increase in competition.

In a survey of 456 global executives, 93 per cent reported that the biggest challenge was the internationalization of competitors, who were becoming more global (Belz *et al.*, 2001). This was followed by the challenge of modifying the organizational structure to serve global customers (85 per cent) and integrating product and service offerings to serve global customers (84 per cent).

Competitive response

In some cases the actions of a specific company within an industry have caused the entire industry to expand globally. For example when

Electrolux, a Swedish consumer appliance manufacturer, entered the US market through the acquisition of White Consolidated, the American white goods company Whirlpool decided to enter the European market through the purchase of Philips' white goods business.

Similar competitive actions have occurred in the alcoholic drinks industry. For example in 1986, when Guinness acquired The Distillers Company, the spirits industry began to see the acquisition of distribution companies as a key success factor and therefore most acquired their key distributors. The spirits industry continued to consolidate. In 1997, Grand Met and Guinness merged to form Diageo. Then in 2000, Diageo and Pernod Ricard acquired and split the Seagrams business, further consolidating the industry (Diageo, 2003).

As a result of competitive actions such as these, a number of companies have determined that they need to be global to remain competitive.

Purchasing processes

Purchasing has become a more important function in most companies. As companies have reengineered their processes to serve customers better, they have recognized the potential value of streamlining the purchasing process to reduce transaction costs, inventory costs and working capital. For example, while General Motors' purchasing strategy ten years ago was initially focused on squeezing suppliers and reducing their margins, the current focus is to develop advanced supply chain management. The increased centralization of purchasing along with the stress on supply chain management has resulted in companies reducing the number of suppliers and often requesting global suppliers.

Canon found that as copying technology moved to digital, the procurement of copiers moved from being a local non-core purchasing practice to a global procurement practice. This global procurement was included in the information technology procurement process, since a copier can additionally be used as a fax, scanner or printer. To respond to this trend, Canon has launched an international account manager programme. The international account managers work with the national sales organization to determine the customer's needs and develop a proposal (Fleming, 1999).

TECHNOLOGY DRIVERS

Convergence of information and communications technologies

The convergence of information technology with telecommunications technology has vastly increased the ability of customers and suppliers to communicate. The communication can be as simple as an e-mail, but could also include real-time replenishment systems where products are ordered and shipped electronically as the consumer purchases them at a retail checkout. Being able to communicate so quickly and easily with customers who are thousands of miles away in different time zones makes commerce much easier than the days of the telex, fax and difficult telephone connections.

Staples, an office products company, sources products from all over the world. Many products come from remote suppliers in smaller Chinese cities. The first requirement for becoming a Staples supplier is to have an active e-mail address.

The Internet

The growth of the Internet has made it possible for suppliers and customers to share information and interact on a global basis, across long geographic distances or many time zones. Sophisticated software for enterprise resource planning (ERP), customer relationship management (CRM) and supply chain management (SCM) allows suppliers to interact and coordinate purchasing globally while reducing transaction and supply chain costs. Finally the impact of e-business, including Internet-based marketplaces, exchanges and auctions, has driven suppliers and customers to identify opportunities for leveraging strategic relationships. With any customer only one or two clicks away via the Internet, the potential methods for customer interaction have changed significantly.

Another benefit of the Internet is in customers' information search process. It allows customers to collect information on many suppliers and quickly compare specification, pricing and availability. Buyers' consequent ability to make more informed decisions increases the potential competition from multiple countries, which has also encouraged many suppliers to develop global offerings.

Speed of product innovation

New products are being developed every day and the innovations seem to come faster and faster. The speed at which new products are entering the market is being matched by the speed at which other companies are imitating the innovations. For example as shown in Table 2.3, the number of new products per year has increased 28 per cent from 24 496 in 1996 to 31 432 in 2000. This overall process requires that companies identify the largest possible available market to get a return on their investment in new products before the imitators enter the market.

Table 2.3 New product introductions

	1996	2000	% increase
Food	11 072	13 373	21
Beverages	3 524	3 541	0
Health and beauty	8 204	11 747	43
Household	782	1 695	116
Pet	444	727	64
Miscellaneous	467	349	−25
TOTAL	24 496	31 432	28

Source: 'New introductions ahead once again in 2000', *Research Alert*, 16 February 2001, p. 7.

CUSTOMERS' RESPONSES TO THE DRIVERS OF GLOBALIZATION

When customers have experienced the macro-economic, market and technology factors that have driven them to consider global business options, they have responded in particular ways to take advantage of the global opportunity. Understanding how companies have responded improves suppliers' understanding of the opportunities for global account management.

Multiple countries

As domestic markets became saturated and traders saw opportunities in other markets they expanded geographically, moving from country to country. Generally companies move to countries that are in close proximity. Sometimes they tended to focus more on countries with a similar language and culture. For example, US companies would expand first to Canada, then to the UK, then to Australia, then to Germany or France.

The normal approach for entering a new market often begins with exporting from the home market. Once sufficient volume has been achieved, companies consider setting up local operations, including manufacturing, marketing, sales and sometimes R&D, to exploit the opportunities in that country in the best way. Companies such as Unilever and Nestlé expanded in many different geographic areas. Over time while serving many smaller markets, companies began to pursue the idea of offering the same product to multiple countries. This of course gave them economies of scale and manufacturing, which reduced manufacturing costs and gave the company a competitive advantage. That leads to the next response of globalization, using company resources across multiple countries.

Use of company resources across multiple countries

As trade barriers for exporting and importing were reduced or eliminated, many companies began to consider a single

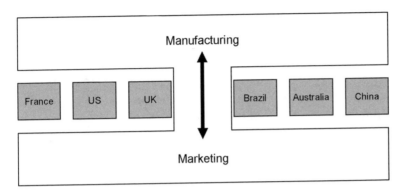

Figure 2.3 Opportunities to leverage manufacturing and marketing across multiple countries

manufacturing facility to serve a group of three or more countries. Developing economies of scale in manufacturing was popular and successful. The ability to leverage manufacturing resources leads companies to consider the possible leveraging of other investments. For example, although there were some benefits in having research and development facilities in every country to tailor the products to local needs, companies quickly found that by centralizing research and development they were able to speed up innovation and development by the consolidation of resources. Companies also began to explore opportunities to leverage their marketing knowledge (Figure 2.3). This initially occurred as marketers became successful with a particular marketing strategy in one country and looked to transfer that success to another country. Success may have been based on a unique product, a specific target market, or possibly the advertising campaign.

Leveraging knowledge from country to country was particularly popular in Europe where there are a large number of countries in close proximity. The barriers to leveraging company resources across multiple countries were often differences in product standards. These could be related to environmental conditions like temperature, or to variations in consumer needs or tastes.

Standardization of products and processes

In 1983 Harvard professor Ted Levitt wrote a classic article in the *Harvard Business Review* on the globalization of markets (Levitt, 1983). He argued that consumer needs around the world were becoming more homogeneous, offering the opportunity for companies to sell the same product in many countries. Levitt further argued that companies who were first able to develop and launch these global products successfully and sell a large volume of products would therefore achieve a significant reduction in production costs, allowing them to lower prices and capture a large market share. This article worried many CEOs, who were concerned that if they didn't develop fully standardized products the globalization train would pass them by. Even though there was significant disagreement with Levitt's views, many companies such as Electrolux, P&G, Ford, General Motors and Black & Decker launched efforts to develop standardized global products.

It was during this rush to globalization that many companies found that they could not develop totally standardized products because consumer needs and environmental conditions varied from market to market. This led some companies to develop platforms based on which more of the product would stay the same, although the exterior of the product would differ from market to market.

Companies also discovered during this process that in many cases the real value of operating in multiple countries was the additional knowledge created in multiple environments. As operations had often grown up on a country-by-country basis, it was difficult to make direct comparisons because the data was reported or collected differently, rendering country-to-country comparisons difficult. Companies found that by standardizing processes such as finance, market research, customer service, customer complaints and new product development, they could more easily make comparisons from market to market and leverage their knowledge in one market more easily in another.

Global purchasing

As companies developed more standardized products and processes, along with standardized information technology systems, they began to share more information from country to country. It immediately came to their notice that they were receiving different levels of support and pricing in different countries from the same manufacturers. Companies also began to explore the possibility of developing global suppliers that would sell to them on a basis of their total global purchases, which would be at a discounted price compared to each individual country purchasing from the same supplier on a country-by-country basis. This led some companies to develop global purchasing departments. Global purchasing allowed them to leverage their buying power, standardize products, reduce transaction costs, reduce the number of suppliers and finally improve the product and service quality demanded from their manufacturers.

The drivers of globalization collectively influence companies to operate in as many countries as possible. As companies expand into multiple countries they often want their suppliers to follow them. For example DSM, a Dutch speciality chemical company that makes elastomers for door seals on automobiles, found that it needed to operate not only in Europe but also in North America, South America and Asia to serve the needs of global car manufacturers adequately.

It is important for suppliers to know their customers' globalization plans, since it is often less risky to expand with current customers rather than to attempt to grow only by acquiring new customers. As companies move into a large number of countries it must quickly be determined which part of their organization they want to leverage across countries versus which part they want to have locally in each country. The determination of global leverage is visualized in Figure 2.4. Research and development is often a function that companies decide to operate centrally. In contrast, it is frequently necessary for suppliers' account managers to be located close to a key customer's headquarters and major R&D sites.

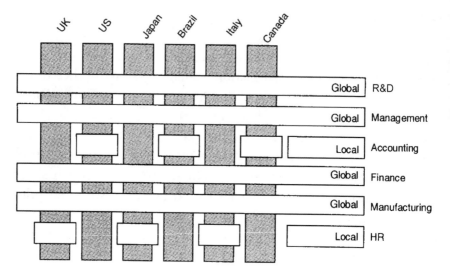

Figure 2.4 Opportunities for global leverage

WHY ESTABLISH A GLOBAL ACCOUNT MANAGEMENT PROGRAMME?

Improve performance

The most important reason for implementing a global account management system is to improve a firm's performance. This additional layer of organizational structure carries an annual cost of approximately $500 000 per global account manager. This estimate includes salary, bonus, benefits, travel expenses, entertainment expenses, secretarial support, training, meetings etc. In some cases the global account manager may replace local or regional positions. To get a return on this investment, a firm needs to increase revenue and profit. A survey of 191 senior international executives from 165 companies found that global account management increased customer satisfaction by 20 per cent, revenues by 15 per cent and profits by 15 per cent (Montgomery & George, 2000).

Procter & Gamble's top six global customers are Ahold, Costco, Carrefour, Wal-Mart, Tesco and Metro/Makro, which together represent 25 per cent of P&G revenue. Its top 50 customers represent 55 per cent of its sales. The goal of P&G's global account management efforts was to develop a new business model to serve large global customers, actively manage global customers, increase the qualifications of the global customer team, increase the company's access to these customers' executive levels and develop specific strategies to add value to global customers. P&G found with its global accounts that it gained through scale, synergies and speed. The global customer benefited from differentiated products and services, tailored marketing concepts and standardized supply chains (Scholl, 2001).

Respond to customer needs

Global customers want global suppliers. They want a single point of contact, pricing based on their global volume, in some cases global pricing, and consistency in terms, such as credit terms, volume discounts and returns policy. They also want a relationship that reflects their importance as a customer. Giving a customer what it wants and needs is usually good practice that leads to an improved position with that customer. The ability to serve global customers should thus lead to increased sales. As global customers grow, so does the business.

Leverage your global resources

As a firm expands with its customers, it will receive the benefit of their established relationships as they enter new countries with existing customers. This reduces the risk of geographic expansion and leverages the investment in a specific customer.

For example Earnest W. Deavenport, Jr., former CEO of Eastman Chemical Company, reported that the company built a resin factory in China to serve the needs of a global customer as well as the China adhesive market. Mr Deavenport said, 'Without the global account management relationship we would not have had the opportunity to follow this customer into a new market' (Deavenport, 1999).

As a supplier develops an information structure to support global customers, this investment can be used with multiple global accounts. Global customers will be able to use the global information system to receive instant answers to questions or product specifications, supply plans and so on. Sharing access to each other's databases and information systems allows both customer and supplier to react more quickly, increasing speed to market and reducing logistics costs.

Develop a competitive advantage

Many industries are becoming more consolidated, with less opportunity for product or service differentiation. A global account management system will allow suppliers to develop competitive advantage. As a supplier helps a customer expand to new markets and identifies ways to create global value for that specific customer, customer loyalty will be strengthened. The global account management deepens the level of understanding and cooperation between supplier and customer, therefore creating a competitive advantage that is difficult for a direct competitor to copy.

Standardization of product and service offerings

As global customers develop global product and service offerings, they want suppliers who can also deliver globally standardized products and services, components, assemblies and sub-assemblies. This standardization concept is pictured in Figure 2.5. Standardization of ingredients and specifications reduces the complexity of the procurement, inventory and production processes, allowing the global customer to make the best use of its investments in research and development, manufacturing and marketing.

The experience of many firms has led to the concept of building new products for global markets on the basis of 'platforms' and 'derivatives'. It is not always possible to offer the exact same product

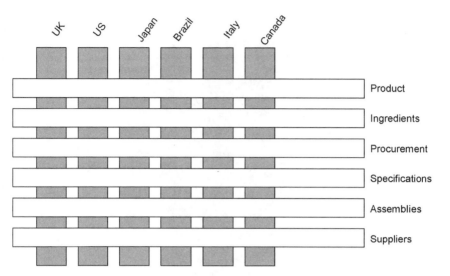

Figure 2.5 Product/service leverage opportunities

in every market due to differences in the end consumer's preferences, language or volume needs, so global customers may develop a standard product platform. This standard platform will be adapted to local needs with different features, packaging or sizes. The product core might be the same for all products in all regions. An extended core might apply for each region but differ across regions. Each region might support one or more basic platforms based on the extended core concept. Finally, each region might launch product derivatives specific to the regional conditions.

This 'platform' strategy allows for different configurations while maintaining a stable product base, thus reducing basic development costs. However, such a global product strategy is possible only if a company has a coherent, well-planned global product development concept. Figure 2.6 illustrates the concept of a core platform with product variants or derivatives for different markets. It is a strategy that continues to provide some manufacturing and R&D economies of scale while tailoring the product to local markets. A key element of this approach is the need to have a common interface between components. For example, National Bicycle of Japan uses modular

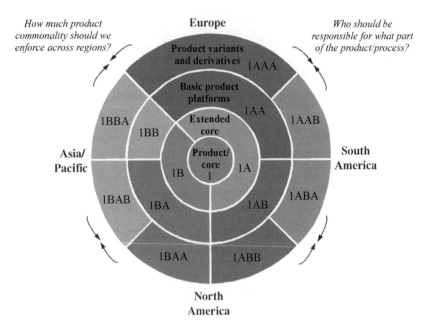

Figure 2.6 Product strategy built around platforms and derivatives

Source: 'Formulating a product strategy', IMD presentation, February 1997.

architecture to provide bicycles that are tailored to the size and body proportions of individual customers. All the connection points are identical to allow easy assembly (Ronchez, 1999).

Hilti Group example

The Hilti Group is a world leader in the development, manufacturing and marketing of value-added top-quality products for professional customers in the construction and building maintenance industries (Hilti, 2001). With a global presence in over 120 countries, 13 780 employees and revenue of 3.1 billion Swiss francs, Hilti's customers are construction firms, distributors, retailers and building maintenance firms. The company has observed that the growth of globalization, improved information technology and development of cohesive economic areas, such as the EU, NAFTA and ASEAN, have led to the following major changes in its customers' needs. Purchasing power is becoming more concentrated, customers are developing professional supply chain management and reducing the number of suppliers, and more subcontracting is being used along with more project-based activities. Further, more customers are increasing usage of the Internet to partner with suppliers and other companies, and finally the overall market is becoming more transparent, allowing for easy comparisons of products, services and pricing.

To cope with the changes in their needs, key suppliers have changed their customer requirements. Customers want suppliers with a geographic reach to mirror their global presence. Customers not only want consistent product offerings globally, but also consistent terms, pricing and customer service. To achieve the required service, customers need a point of contact who is accountable for coordinated business relationships, as well as a strategic and operational fit. To deliver on these customer needs, Hilti has built a global account management programme that contributes to its global accounts' productivity by providing exclusive use of a worldwide customized hardware and software system, cooperating on construction projects from design to completion, and offering a globally coordinated multi-level customer approach (Hilti, 2001).

CONCLUSION

As the world economy becomes more stable and interdependent, world trade will continue to grow faster than domestic GNP. The saturation of domestic markets, the deregulation of industries, the privatization of government-run firms and the opening of other markets like China and India have all contributed to the global growth of firms. As firms pursue global opportunities through acquisition, expansion and partnerships, they want global suppliers for their key products. Global account management is the best way to respond to the needs of global customers by coordinating and focusing resources on their needs.

Analysing a Global Customer's Industry   3

Understanding your customer begins with an understanding of the industry in which it operates. Over the last decade, the type of analysis that companies undertake has changed significantly. Typically companies conducted a competitive analysis on other firms offering similar or competing products or services. Any firm directly encountered in the market became the focus of analysis. This type of market view analysis was very detailed in comparing directly competitive product offerings. In order to know a competitor, managers prepared detailed lists of different product features and prices, and compared customer reactions to the various product offerings (Kotler & Armstrong, 2000). The process of competitive analysis helped a firm understand possible strategies to improve its offerings versus those of known competitors.

In the early 1980s this traditional form of competitive analysis gave way to the industry view (Kotler & Armstrong, 2000). The industry view was based on gaining insights from analysing an entire industry, and was viewed as a departure from traditional competitive analysis (Kotler, 2002). The main proponent of industry-based competitive analysis was Porter, who published two seminal books, *Competitive Strategy* and *Competitive Advantage*. The focus of the analysis became an entire industry, including all relevant participants, both upstream and downstream, for a given set of industry competitors. The analysis called for a much more comprehensive view and included several types of industry participants that were not part of the traditional competitive analysis (Porter, 1980).

With this different, and more coherent, view of an entire industry, a rich set of insights could be gained that deal with the dynamics of an industry, eventually leading to an understanding of the basic requirements to be met by all competitors. These basic requirements, which we will later revisit under the name of key success factors (KSFs), are essential building blocks towards the understanding of competitive strategies.

Typically, such analysis tended to be left to corporate strategists and was not viewed as part of the job description of account management. A basic and underlying assumption is the authors' strong belief that the development of successful global account strategies requires an account team fully to absorb the customer's industry dynamics.

Furthermore, the industry view of the competitive struggle yields important insights as to the role that global account management can and should play as part of an integrated marketing strategy. It is therefore absolutely essential that account managers learn to apply the industry view and to incorporate its conclusions into building competitive global account strategies.

THE MACRO BUSINESS SYSTEM

The basic building block of understanding an industry is the macro business system. It includes all industry participants connected in a successive chain of value-adding units, starting from raw materials and moving downstream to OEM (original equipment manufacturer) customers, wholesalers, retailers and customers or end users. In many situations it also includes the recycling stage. Just as in macro-economics, where macro denotes the study of the behaviour of the economy as a whole, the term 'macro business systems' applies to an entire industry with all the relevant participants represented in the value-added stream, both up and downstream, from the point of view of a given customer (Samuelson & Nordhaus, 1989).

We are thus defining the macro business system, shown in Figure 3.1, as an industry's value chain (Porter, 1985). Later on we will examine the micro business system, which is the value chain within

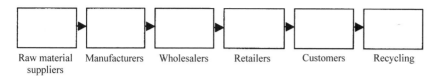

Figure 3.1 Macro business system

the company, consisting of value-added steps and processes as they take place within a firm. This is consistent with Porter's definition of the firm value chain (Porter, 1985). However, since the type of analysis gained from understanding the macro business system differs from the analysis of the micro business system, we are beginning with the macro view of the industry.

PARTICIPANTS IN THE MACRO BUSINESS SYSTEM

Participants in the macro business system are those participants, or groups of companies, that directly participate in the flow of goods as they move from primary raw materials to finished products and to customers and/or consumers. The number of different stages present in a macro business system depends on the prevalent industry structure and the extent to which one finds freestanding activities among independent firms. For any stage in a macro value chain represented by a significant number of independent entities, a separate stage or participant category needs to be considered for analysis.

Although we can speak of a standard business system (see above), it will be clear to any experienced analyst that each industry offers its own challenges and consists of its own unique business system. The participant categories will differ among industries, and the type and numbers of participating groups will vary. The methodology, however, is consistent. It requires flow charting of the value-added stream of an industry and identifying each step that is normally represented by an independent group of firms.

The starting point of any industry analysis would be the definition of an industry. This has been a preoccupation of writers in the past. Traditional marketing theory has tended to approach industry analysis from a business definition point of view (Abell & Hammond, 1979). The use of the term 'business' has given way to the term 'industry', with business more often referred to as an organizational unit. However, both recent and classical writers have accepted the fact that drawing the line around an industry, defining its boundaries, and thus determining the elements part of it, are as much an art as a science.

For the purpose of this book, we thus define an industry as the set of interrelated activities and organizational units that are part of a value chain activity. As has been recommended, an industry is more than merely a segment (Porter, 1985). It incorporates all those participants that contribute to serving the demand constituted by a coherent group of segments, or markets, for which one set of participants is the main source of satisfaction.

Looking at some industry examples, we could say that construction toys, such as those manufactured by LEGO, are part of the construction toy segment, which is part of the broader toy industry, as are games, dolls and other toy products. Expensive luxury watches, such as those made by Rolex, are part of the watch industry, and fashion watches made by Swatch are part of the same industry. It is clear, however, that the boundaries are not always neatly defined and that judgement is involved as to what or who is part of one industry and where the next industry starts. In our opinion, when a separate set of participants consistently competes in only one part of an industry and not in another, a new industry may begin. Again, carefully tracing the flow of products, components and technology would indicate if we were dealing with a separate value-added chain.

TYPICAL CATEGORIES AND INDUSTRY PARTICIPANTS

No two industry business systems are likely to look exactly the same. Although most industry business systems will consist of a certain category of players, each industry is likely to call for its own specific categorization, labelling and flow patterns. The main categories that we expect to find are suppliers, manufacturers, intermediate users

(OEMs), wholesalers, retailers, customers and an increasing number of recyclers. Let us examine each of these typical participants.

There is usually a multitude of different supplier categories in one industry, often comprising many different materials or components. In product industries, a useful approach is to list the key components that make up a particular industry product. In the watch industry, major categories of components are watch movements, bracelets, casings, dial and face. In the case of automobiles we have a range of different components, such as tyres, glass, electronics, axles, braking systems and lighting systems. Both industries, however, have component flows into the product manufacturing/assembly stage. In many process industries we have materials, rather than components. For paint, we have key materials such as resins, solvents, pigments and other additives. In either case, these components or raw materials make up the relevant supply stage of an industry, as shown in Figure 3.2.

How far back into the raw material chain one needs to analyse depends on the structure of the supplying industries. When a certain supply industry serves largely one group of manufacturers or processors only, the inclusion for strategic analysis is obvious. Once the suppliers are shared between different manufacturing groups with different customers that typically do not compete, it may not become

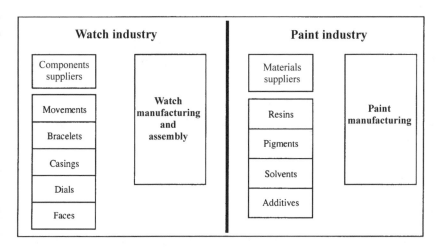

Figure 3.2 Material/component portion of the macro business system

necessary to analyse suppliers further back in the value chain. The key is therefore the extent to which a certain group of manufacturers absorbs a given group of suppliers' output.

Manufacturers and processors

Manufacturers and processors are the main producers of an industry's output. They include all the steps of an industry's value chain and can be identified by following the physical flow of goods or processes along an entire industry. For our analysis, we need to capture the separate groups of manufacturers. If several steps are routinely combined under the same group of competitors, no further subdivision will be needed. However, in industries where there are separate, freestanding firms and integrated companies, both steps would be required for independent analysis.

An example is the paint industry, where we have both merchant suppliers of resins to all paint companies and larger paint companies that manufacture part of their own resins, a key raw material for paint. Similarly in the watch industry, independent firms supply some components while integrated firms use captive suppliers.

Secondary users or OEMs

In many industries products are marketed through secondary users or OEMs (original equipment manufacturers). This is true for most car components such as tyres, as shown in Figure 3.3, which are supplied to OEMs, or car manufacturers, and then sold to dealers and on to consumers. Where such a stage in the business system is present, it needs to be evaluated carefully with respect to influence, both backwards and forwards.

Wholesalers

Wholesalers are considered as part of the macro business system to the extent that they exist as independent firms. In some industries

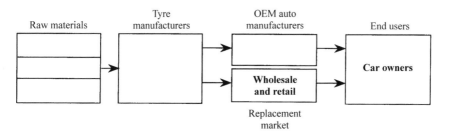

Figure 3.3 Macro business system of car component manufacturers (tyres)

manufacturers perform their own wholesaling functions through branch sales points. In this case, these sales branches are part of the previous stage in the value chain and are not broken out separately.

Depending on the industry, wholesalers may be known by various labels, for example they might be called distributors. Independent wholesalers have been on the defensive in many industries and rarely account for the entire volume of an industry. Instead, this group of macro industry participants shares its role with either retailers or manufacturers.

Retailers

For products marketed to consumers, retailers are an integral part of the macro industry business system. Depending on the industry, there are different classes of retailers. For fast-moving consumer goods (FMCGs), supermarkets, discounters and hypermarkets are important retailers. For automobiles, the local car dealer is representative of the retail stage.

Consumers and end users

The final stage in most business systems is made up of consumers or, in the case of consumption goods, the individual consumers and families. 'End user' is a term that we use more frequently in business-to-business marketing. Although it may be appropriate to use the term 'customer', we have found that this terminology is often misleading. Many companies refer to the customer as the group of firms next in line in the business system, which are often intermediaries, not the consumer or end user.

Recyclers

Recyclers often make up the last stage in a macro business system. With the emergence of environmental concerns as a major element for many industries, products no longer 'end' at the consumption stage. Under recycling we include all activities to reclaim part of or the entire product. For some industries this may mean professionally managed and licensed landfills. Increasingly, recyclers collect and take back consumer products such as packaging materials (PET bottles, glass bottles, paper etc.). Government regulations in parts of Europe and the US have also mandated such activities for industrial products. It has therefore become necessary to include recycling in the analysis of the dynamics of a macro business system.

DEVELOPING DIFFERENT MAPS OF MACRO BUSINESS SYSTEMS

Analysing an industry in depth can yield different types of value chain. One of the main difficulties for the analyst is to avoid succumbing to the view that all macro industry business systems look alike. Instead, we can identify a number of prototype macro business systems.

Secondly, the analyst needs to make sure that a company's own value chain focusing on a global account does not get confused with the value chain of the account itself. For many business services, the service does not become part of the value chain of the account. Likewise, capital equipment, as well as supplies used in either production or administration, does not become part of the value stream. If a supplying firm took a narrow view of an account, it might confuse its own value chain with that of the customer and

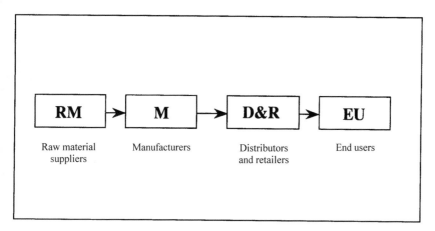

Figure 3.4 Standard business system

draw limiting conclusions. To avoid such confusion, we will explain several different types of macro business systems.

The standard business system

The standard type of business system, shown in Figure 3.4, consists of raw material suppliers, manufacturers, distributors and customers/end users. Although it is helpful to illustrate the concept of the business system in a simple version, reality is such that most industries are more complex and will require the analyst to think more creatively about the value-creating flow. The standard business system view is appropriate for firms supplying components or raw materials that become part of their global account's own products.

The multi-stage business system

Increasingly we are encountering industries where the value-creation chain consists of several distinct stages or participants, thus leading to the term 'multi-stage'. In the multi-stage business system, as shown in Figure 3.5, there may be several steps of raw material suppliers as well as several intermediate users. Excellent examples of multi-stage

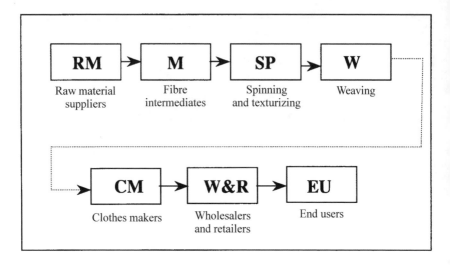

Figure 3.5 Multi-stage business system: textile fibres

industries are textiles, where the raw material (cotton, manmade fibres) travels through a number of value-creation steps, all structured as independent groups of industry participants, ending with the garment manufacturers and retailers.

The 'T' business system

Although most marketers might find themselves in a standard/multi-stage business system, this is appropriate only where the output of the previous stage is consumed in the next stage. This is true for many materials or consumables. However, the reality of the equipment or industrial equipment industries is quite different. The builders of textile weaving machinery do not see their machines become part of the end product (textile cloth or clothing). Their business 'ends' with the textile-weaving firms. In return, textile weavers do not consider machines as 'raw material'. Consequently, we need to think of the business system as a 'T' where the raw material flow is on one axis (textiles, cloth, paper etc.) and the machinery on the perpendicular axis, as illustrated in Figure 3.6.

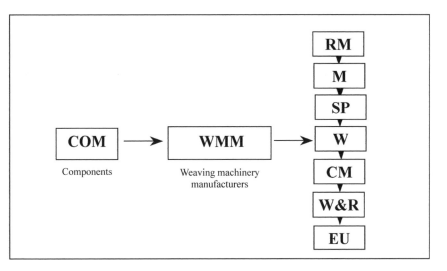

Figure 3.6 'T' business system: textile/weaving machinery

It is important, however, to recognize that the major dynamics of the business system usually emanate from the raw material 'T', thus dominating the realities of equipment manufacturers. For industrial equipment marketers, therefore, it is of great importance to recognize the 'T' business system as different from the traditional one.

The parallel business system

In circumstances where materials or products can be substituted, the most insightful way to look at the macro industry is the parallel business system, shown in Figure 3.7. Let's use packaging materials as an example. A maker of steel cans supplying a packer of canned food products needs to be aware of the existence of a parallel industry system of glass, laminates or other packaging materials. All aimed at the same decision point, the packer has to make a selection from among the available materials streams.

The dynamics of a parallel business system are thus of great importance to many chemicals and material firms, but also regarding some industrial components where an OEM may be able to make

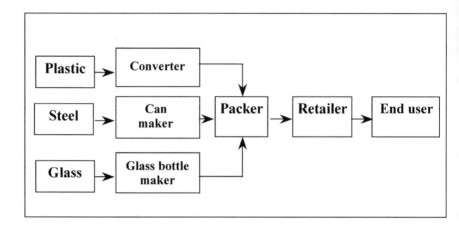

Figure 3.7 Parallel business system: metal can industry

trade-offs between different technical solutions from two different streams of industry value chains. Here, the process of substitution among competing parallel business systems governs the competitive forces.

The star business system

One of the most complex types of business system is that characterized by such terms as 'the office of the future' or 'the factory of the future'. In these situations, the 'future' is not yet a product. Instead, we are dealing with different configurations of important components that need to be integrated into one system.

In the case of the factory of the future, the components include machine tools, transfer systems, robots, computer controls, inventory controls and so on. If analysed, each of those components is actually making up its own industry and can be configured as its own macro business system. Due to the complexity of the factory of the future, each of those business systems aims at the manufacturer/client where the components are combined into a modern manufacturing system. Competitively, each group of participants hopes to become

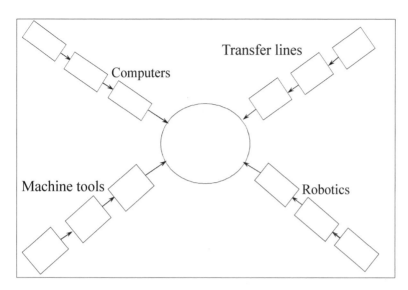

Figure 3.8 Star business system

the 'power broker' by assuming key control over the decision-making process and specifications. Whoever controls the specifications or interfaces between parties will be able to 'spec' others in or out and essentially emerge as the key power.

It is therefore important to understand the dynamics of the star system shown in Figure 3.8 as different from the realities of some of the other systems we have identified. The star system is of primary importance to suppliers of complex industrial systems.

The circular business system

Thus far we have tended to view business systems primarily as a one-way flow from upstream activities through to downstream activities, ending with an end user. In many industries, however, the flow of value added or materials does not finish with the end user. Instead, through recycling we have found a way to reuse materials. Such recycling flows are already at a very high volume for paper (newsprint in particular) and steel. In both industries the amount of material recycled is in direct competition with virgin material coming

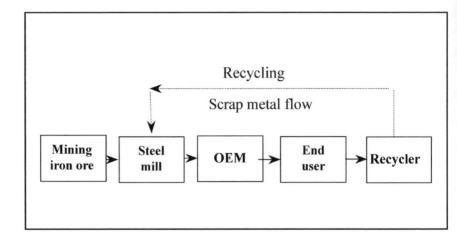

Figure 3.9 Circular business system

from either paper mills or integrated steel mills. It can be expected that the 'take back' portion of many other industries will increase and that most industries will contain a circular system for a portion of usage, although in most it will not reach the extent of either paper or steel. The circular system for the steel industry is shown in Figure 3.9.

ANALYSING BUSINESS SYSTEMS FOR SERVICE INDUSTRIES

One of the most challenging assignments is to develop a macro business system for a service industry. In contrast to the physical value chains in the product sector, for services we have much greater difficulty following a chain of steps and identifying discrete groups of participants since we do not have a physical flow of goods. Nevertheless, this does not mean that business system analysis is not valid for service industries. Instead, the analysis will have to take different forms and what is included in a given industry business system for a service industry is likely to follow different rules.

Analysing flows may still be the most appropriate way to draw boundary lines for a service industry. The flows are not products or materials, but can contain different elements. Developing an industry from customer flows may be appropriate for the airline and healthcare industries; in the latter, patients are the equivalent of the passengers for airlines. Tracing money flows is a starting point in the banking industry and many financial services industries. For other industries such as credit cards, using information flows may illustrate a good picture of the industry business system. Paper flows may be appropriate in the insurance industry and, finally, physical flow of goods (in the form of packages) may lead to an appropriate industry business system in the courier and transport business.

The challenge for service industries is to chart a business system that, although different in composition and steps, lends itself to the same type of analysis as for manufacturing industries. We firmly believe that this type of analysis applied to service industries yields as much in terms of rich insights as when applied to manufacturing industries. Throughout this chapter we will therefore apply our concepts to both. However, in instances where the service industry offers particular challenges that require an innovative analytical approach, we will separately note those instances and hope to supply and suggest some of these innovative approaches.

CONCLUSIONS FROM ANALYSING A CUSTOMER'S INDUSTRY

The purpose of developing a clear picture of the macro business system faced by a strategic client stems from the need to analyse further this system for key managerial insights. It is these insights that greatly enhance the client relationship and shape the client's view of the supplier or global account manager.

Here are some of the insights or conclusions that can be drawn from the macro business system analysis. Clearly, in the context of a book on global account management we do not have the luxury of detailing these concepts to the same extent as we might as a strategist or consultant. Nevertheless, global account managers need to develop an insider's view of their client's industry environment to gain clout and access.

Creating strategic groups

Assuming that the focus of the analysis is the next industry participant group downstream from the global account manager, industry participants need to be clustered into similar strategic groups following similar generic strategies. Although some generic groups are frequently cited, such as low cost, focus or differentiation, we would encourage account managers to group the participants creatively into categories that may be dedicated to a given industry rather than using standard groups for any industry (Porter, 1985).

The basis for clustering competitors into different strategic groups is the creative process and would occur around different variables depending on an industry. In the pharmaceutical industry, relevant clustering can occur around the research-driven players vs the generic players, and even among the research-driven players are some that are aiming at several therapeutic categories vs those that target only a few categories. In other industries, clustering might occur around the choice of integration, the breadth of segment selection, the extent of global reach or the scope of businesses combined into a single strategy. Clearly, an interesting strategic grouping is more than what the target client uses in its own strategy and should reflect some original thinking on the part of the global account management team.

Learning lessons from winners and losers

An important element of sizing up industry behaviour comes from grouping industry participants into 'winners' and 'losers'. Since the account management team is challenged to have strategic insights about the industry where its global client competes, it is important to learn lessons from observing winning behaviour vs losing behavior. Winning companies invariably tell us about industry practices that lead towards success, and losing companies harbour lessons for us to learn so that the types of choices made and strategies executed by them will be avoided. Both groups of participants are needed for serious insights into any industry.

This classification would be based on the success of competing strategies over time, and not on market size or market share alone. Winners are companies that have gained share, tend to be of above-average industry profitability and are generally viewed as practice leaders as well. A typical industry participants may be included in this analysis for more interesting and richer feedback. Losers are firms at the opposite end of the scale of the above dimensions.

Defining industry economics and 'metrics'

Each industry has its relevant economics or financial realities. Understanding the cost structure of the industry and its impact on success is important for strategic assessment. Industries have particular financial footprints resulting in given asset structures, asset intensities and overall profitability. Many of these elements are similar for all companies.

Most industries also operate around key ratios, or measurements, that are of overriding importance for all players. In retailing, for instance, profitability per square foot or cubic foot is such a metric. A global account manager who aspires to a deep understanding of his or her client's industry needs to be able to isolate these metrics, whether they are of a financial or operational nature. Some of them are used widely by industry participants, whereas others may just be emerging and may be new to a given industry.

Performing a strategic segmentation

The final 'block' on the industry business system tends to contain the relevant customer (end user) groups. The market is typically segmented and reflects different parts of the overall industry. Segments occur along different dimensions: product, technology, customer groups, industry users, applications, company size, geography etc.

Unless special effort is undertaken, account marketing teams tend to segment their direct customers (or accounts) into different categories. The typical approach centres on buying criteria or other behavioural models that categorize customers by different purchasing criteria. For insightful analysis of global or major accounts, teams will have to drill down to the end of the industry business system and segment the customers' customers, or end users.

When performing a strategic segmentation, the market is categorized into the main industry sectors. These categories tell us more about how the market is structured, and less about the classic marketing segmentation where segments reflect particular buyer behaviour along narrower lines. For example in the paint industry, the strategic segments consist of user categories such as decorative paint for buildings, paint for the automotive industry as purchased by OEMs or car manufacturers, paint for refinishing cars in need of repairs, or coatings used on the interior of tin cans in the food and beverage industry. This differs from the more classic marketing segmentation where segments might consist of different decorative segments marketed through stores, to professionals and so on, and where segments would be used to help define more detailed customer groups for the purpose of directing marketing operations.

For purposes of this analysis, we have added a figure depicting strategic segmentation of the world paint industry along three main dimensions: user industries, paint technologies and geography, as

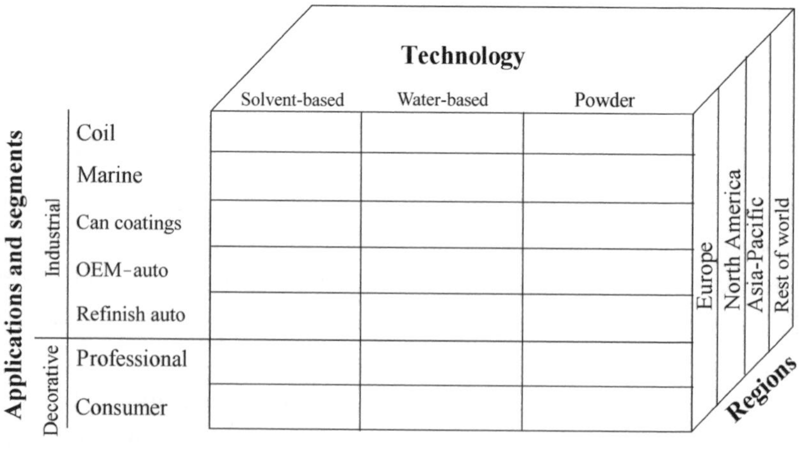

Figure 3.10 Strategic segmentation

illustrated in Figure 3.10. Obtaining clarity concerning the relevant strategic segmentation will be important when probing for industry trends, as we shall see later in this chapter.

DEVELOPING STRATEGIC INSIGHTS BY CRACKING THE INDUSTRY CODE

Once the account team has assembled the necessary data to lay out a client's industry business system, the next step is to extract the key lessons from the analysis. What every account team needs to learn is its client's requirements for success in a given industry. To some extent the account team needs to 'crack the code of the industry' containing the key success factors or basic competitive requirements to succeed. An account team cannot really claim to understand the client's business until it has determined the industry code.

The industry code is the behaviour required from a participant to assure long-term success. It must be met to achieve profitability and success. Implied in this language is the understanding that violating the industry code would endanger a business's profitability. An industry can have more than one code, such as individual codes for each strategic segment. Where multiple codes exist, some part of the code might apply to multiple segments or sectors, and others might be relevant only for a part of the industry.

To be useful the code needs to contain an industry's imperatives, which are a collection of 'musts' or things that a company must do. These are different from mere core competencies, which describe what a company does well. Imperatives are important for a company to know because they must be observed for long-term success.

Included in the industry code are key success factors, which are the basic competitive requirements that an industry participant has to master for long-term success. Typically, KSFs describe basic actions, or industry behaviours, that winning companies must master. We categorize KSFs into qualifiers, which determine if a participant is able to 'play' in an industry, and differentiators, KSFs that can set players apart from others. All industry participants need to comply with the qualifiers, but only some players may perform on differentiators.

CONTENT OF AN INDUSTRY CODE

For an industry code to be of value, it must answer some important questions that relate to the competitive behaviour in that industry. Below we list some typical imperatives as part of a code, but each industry is likely to have unique aspects. Here are some of the more frequently cited elements of an industry code:

- 'Must segment(s)' are those in which a competitor needs to be present to be a major player. Based on the strategic segmentation described earlier, an analysis of the industry will yield some understanding of such must segments. They are important because of their relative size, their above-average profitability, or their growth and technical development. Once must segments have been identified, every leading player should be in those sectors.
- 'Must combinations' or bundles of segments represent the next level of understanding. In many industries companies do not have a choice of only being in one segment. Frequently they need to be in several segments, and then the particular choice of segments becomes an important issue. A company needs to be able to assess the bundle of segments that best fits its requirements.
- The minimum amount of market coverage to reach strategic goals is also a strategic conclusion that comes from understanding the industry code. For example, a company needs to have access to, say, 60 per cent of the total market opportunity to be a leader, but it could reach its strategic objective with less (or might need more).
- Critical mass, a frequently cited notion in many industries, can be of prime importance. Described as the minimum size required to be competitive or successful, critical mass is difficult to assess because the definition is not apparent. Critical mass may occur around a

company's entire volume, or may be more relevant if assessed by segment, country or geographic unit, key function (such as minimum R&D budget) or another part of a company's business. Again, deep understanding and appreciation of the industry's relevant critical mass come from the above analysis.

- Required level of integration can be important in some industries. The industry code may require different levels of integration to be successful. Forward integration deals with the ownership or control of the downstream part of the industry. Backward integration concerns the upstream aspects of ownership or control. Understanding the relevant amount of integration, and its impact on industry profitability, is an important part of sizing up the industry.
- Required focus, or restrictions on selected activities, can be an important part of the industry code in most industries. The important job of the analyst is to figure out where firms should focus. Focus dimensions might include integration levels, range of products, range of segments, geographic spread, range of technologies and so on.
- Strategic dilemmas are critical questions facing company CEOs and cause senior executives to lose sleep at night. One of the frequently asked questions when dealing with global account teams is how a team may develop an understanding of the strategic dilemmas. Clearly, insights that are readily available, or learned directly from the client's contacts, are not as valuable as those obtained independently and viewed as additional value added by the client. If an account team wants to do more than read up on an industry, answering a few key questions will help shape a proprietary view of the client's industry.
- In connection with the industry's development, assessing the major dilemmas faced by industry participants could contribute to your proprietary view of the client's industry and the challenges facing the client. Dilemmas manifest themselves through choices or decisions to be made or determining which 'forks in the road' to take. Dilemmas could be centred on

forward or backward integration, segment focus, bundles of segments, mastering of single or multiple technologies and so on.

Globalizing the industry code: global logic (imperatives)

Particularly for firms targeted for global account teams, the relevant global imperative (global logic) in an industry is part of the overall analysis. Global logic expresses the intensity of the global rationale, be it from the industry customers, competitors, size or economies of scale, purchasing behaviour or other relevant business reasons (Jeannet, 2000). Because of the importance of global logic, Chapter 4 will be devoted to this topic.

Global chessboard

When looking at the opportunity in a given industry, it is advisable to view it in terms of the entire global opportunity, not merely in terms of one single market such as the US or Europe. Again, we use the chessboard metaphor in explaining the dynamics of global opportunity (Jeannet & Hennessey, 2001). When we depict the entire global opportunity in the form of a chessboard, each country assumes a certain size depending on the importance of its market. The global chessboard is thus not a typical chessboard with 64 equal-sized squares, it consists of some 200 different markets with each market, or country, represented by a different-sized 'square'. Since the global opportunity for each industry is differently distributed across the world, the particular shape of the chessboard is industry specific. When performing a macro industry analysis, it is important to be cognizant of the shape of that industry's chessboard in order to ensure that the data set, vision and perspective remain global throughout the analysis. An illustration of the world as a global chessboard is shown in Figure 3.11, where each country is depicted as a percentage of world national income.

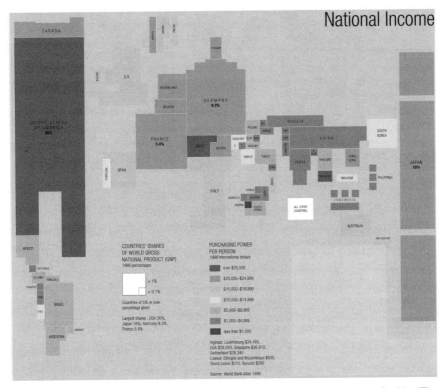

Figure 3.11 Global chessboard. Reprinted with permission from Dan Smith, *The State of the World Atlas*, 6th edition. Copyright ©Myriad Editions Limited

Industry vision

The industry vision captures the future track of the industry and with a complete analysis would lead to the future industry business system structure. This is important, since industry participants are heavily influenced by this development. Part of the industry vision occurs when examining emerging industry code(s), metrics, fault lines and so on to provide a forward-looking understanding of an industry.

Industry 'fault lines'

Fault lines are areas around which there is a major shift in an industry. They might be around winning or losing segments, winning or losing technologies, shifts in customer preferences, shifts in market

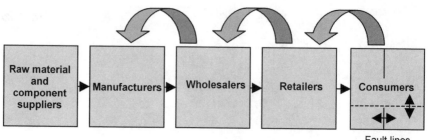

Figure 3.12 Business system ripple effect

geographies etc. Fault lines tend to signal potential changes in the industry business system, or highlight changes caused by external forces (new technologies, government regulations or political groups such as NGOs). Identifying such fault lines will help focus the analysis and make the key account team more aware of where significant developments might occur.

Changes emanating from industry fault lines have a 'ripple effect' in the macro business system, as illustrated in Figure 3.12. Once an effect has been established, a thoughtful observer can anticipate the effects across multiple stages in the business system. In particular, effects starting downstream, such as among the end user or customer base, have the potential of mirroring backwards to the beginning of a macro business system. Fault line identification thus serves as a process for spotting and anticipating such changes.

ANALYSING THE DYNAMICS OF THE MACRO BUSINESS SYSTEM

The purpose of examining the macro business system is not to end up with a complicated design that represents the value-added flow in a given industry. Rather, it is to understand the macro business system faced by a given company rooted in the important dynamics present and their impact on business activities. If a company wants to create value for its customers, it needs to have a fundamental understanding of what the key developments in the industry are, since they will eventually result in changes in the way companies market their products and services.

The outcome of such an analysis will yield a much clearer understanding of what will happen to each industry participant in the future and how the complex web of inter-relationships will change. From the point of view of global account management, we are particularly interested in making the analysis relevant with respect to value creation opportunities. However, in a broad sense we must first understand what the key developments are and how they affect the way business is being conducted at each stage of an industry.

With an understanding of the macro business system, the industry code and dilemmas facing the industry, the global account team will have an excellent perspective on that industry. We will now explain a series of additional elements that can be analysed in relation to a given industry. This is not a complete list; rather, it is meant as a start and such an inquiry would lead to further analysis uncovering underlying trends in an industry.

Developments

Most industries can be described by outlining the status quo and by tracing and defining their business system, which will highlight the current key relationships. However, it is much more important to see changes, since they will invariably force all industry participants to adjust their strategies. Looking for important changes in the future or a different emphasis for a business is a starting point. These changes may come from government legislation, environmental requirements, technological breakthroughs, new and emerging markets or changing competitive structures. Wherever the changes arise, the macro business system of an industry needs to be analysed with respect to the important changes that can reasonably be expected to take place.

The automobile industry serves as an excellent example. In the late 1980s, management at the Philips Automotive Entertainment Division, which develops all types of car radios and stereo systems, was facing a change in the way it did business. Historically, automotive companies and customers had had very low expectations of car radios. Radios tended to look alike and similar radios were sold to various car companies. With the advent of energy-efficient cars, car manufacturers were submitting their models to extensive wind tunnel tests in an effort to reduce drag and thus energy consumption. This resulted in the external car shapes looking more and more similar. When trying to differentiate these cars, companies found the dashboard an important element. Since car radios were mounted on dashboards, their design suddenly became a very important element. Car manufacturers no longer wanted to have similarity in design, forcing car radio manufacturers into a system of offering differently designed radios for each of their key clients.

This example serves as an illustration of how a particular development, in this case energy savings, rippled through an entire industry and affected the operations of other industry participants. Identifying such changes in an industry is one of the more challenging aspects in developing a strategy for a business. Sometimes these changes come rather slowly in the form of industry shifts (Gilbert & Strebel, 1989), while at other times they may be perceived as abrupt and as breakpoints (Strebel, 1992). The following section illustrates various techniques for further refining industry analysis.

When important change factors have a major effect on an industry, they become change drivers. These drivers are the key factors that make or force change in the macro business system. In his widely circulated work *Competitive Advantage*, Porter distinguishes five principal forces that shape industry dynamics: industry rivalry, new entrants, alternative technologies, buyer power and supplier power (Porter, 1985). These forces directly affect the bargaining power of the various players in an industry. We need to recognize that these forces apply to any stage of the macro business system and therefore a detailed analysis could be performed for any participant group that we had earlier defined as being part of our industry business system.

Before we consider these forces, it is important to understand the underlying drivers for an industry. Four sources of drivers can be identified and are found in most industries: technology, economics, changes in customer composition and new entrants.

Technology is perhaps the easiest underlying driver to understand, although it is not always easy to detect. The computer industry offers an excellent example of changes in technology and its pervasive effect on all industry participants. Up until the early 1980s, the large mainframe computers holding and processing vast amounts of information were the leading installations in most firms and their corporate electronic data processing (EDP) departments. In the mid-1970s they were challenged by mini computers, which essentially performed the same function but were smaller-scale machines for 'departmental processing'. In the 1980s, the advent of the ever more powerful personal computer enabled distributed processing. The arrival of the microprocessor made it possible to pack even more computing power into small personal computers. The resulting development of client servers that held application programs accessed by large numbers of personal computers radically changed the structure of the computer industry. Today, the restructuring of IBM and other mainframe suppliers is largely caused by this technological change. Similar technological changes occur in other industries. For example, the move from mechanical to electronic watches was a major technology change affecting the entire industry.

Technological changes come in various forms: they may consist of technology breakthroughs embodied in design, materials or processes. While design changes tend to be associated mostly with new patents and forms of products, both material changes and process changes have an important impact as well. Many industries associated with chemicals or metals have experienced such changes. An example is the development of plastic materials that suddenly can perform better than steel or aluminium. Processes in some industries can have a major impact, such as the expected change in the beer-brewing process as a result of biotechnology developments that result in different or better yeast. For other industries changes in information technology ranging from telecommunications to computers have greatly affected the industry structure. The availability of cheaper and faster telecommunications has affected many industries that depend on information technology.

Often overlooked in technology analysis are the technologies of competing industries. Referred to as substitutes by Porter, they may become more competitive as a result of technology changes even when the industry under scrutiny does not face any particular changes (Porter, 1985). Substitutes, which must be scrupulously analysed when we are facing parallel industry business systems, are more difficult to assess because of the not-invented-here-syndrome that often makes such breakthroughs appear less relevant.

Industry economics and changes are of major concern to all industry participants. Under industry economics we understand the existing cost structure at the overall industry level and for each of the player groups, as well as the critical mass requirements that lead to ideal unit size. These factors are determined by some of the cost drivers, such as economies of scale, learning curve, experience curve and the fixed cost vs variable cost structure of an industry.

At the outset, the analysis should yield a complete picture of the value added by the key player groups in the macro business system. This step is best approached by asking how much the end user pays for a given product or service, and by allocating that price or expenditure among the various industry participant groups. Once the value added for each group is determined, the analysis must also include estimates of the cost structure of the various players. This practice is not common among market analysts. Estimates must be established for the cost structure of suppliers, manufacturers, distributors/retailers and customers (OEMs). This includes understanding both the fixed cost vs variable cost structure in that industry and the scale effects (Brimson, 1991).

Cost dynamics are often insufficiently analysed. Scale effects can accrue either across an entire company or per plant. In the case of many chemical process industries, the relevant scale is the processing plant and its output or tonnage, and the overall total output of the company is secondary. In car manufacturing, not only the overall unit output counts but it is per model composition that determines profitability. When analysing cost structure, the fundamental question to be asked is how cost advantages or scale accrue. It is also important to understand the unit of relevant cost accumulation (plant, model, product line, total output worldwide, segment volume etc.).

The cost structure of all industry participants needs to be understood. Component suppliers and product manufacturers or processors have a different cost structure than OEMs or distributor/ wholesalers or retailers. In the past, account management tended to focus more on downstream players such as distributors/retailers in consumer goods or OEMs in industrial marketing settings. As we will see, this limited view must make room for a broader view of industry economics that includes all other player groups.

Cost structure analysis leads to the clarification of critical size, or the minimal size for effective competition in an industry. In many industries, a minimal size for effective and profitable operations does exist. In the car industry it is generally believed that an assembly plant needs an output of some 200 000 cars annually. Similar output constraints exist in other industries. Often the constraint is a function of a key strategic element, such as a new generation of technology, that occurs in one fixed step and, if a company wants to continue, it must expand in order to stay with competitors. Such fixed-cost elements often shape minimal size or the required volume that a company must have to stay in the game. Cost analysis, both of fixed-cost and variable-cost components, is therefore important. Not only does today's cost structure need to be understood but also the structure of the future, since many industry trends may be triggered by changing cost structures.

New entrants also shape the dynamics of an industry. Competitors entering an industry can do so at all stages: at the raw material stage, as manufacturers, as distributors and so on. Such new entrants may be attracted to a highly profitable industry or, more frequently, may enter with new technology. The paint industry has seen considerable technology changes, going from solvent-based to water-based paint and most recently to powder paint. Most of the key players in powder paint were not previously in wet paint and can thus be considered as new players. Tracing some of the most recent entrants in an industry can help develop a picture or pattern. What we need to analyse, however, is the impact of these new entrants on the major players' operations. Simply stating that they are present is not sufficient to enhance our understanding of an industry.

Finally, changes in customer composition are another strong source of industry dynamics. These are changes in the number, size or needs of users or segments. Since we will be spending a considerable amount of time on segmentation and understanding market structures, at this point we will briefly mention that these developments, sometimes in combination with technology, industry economics and new entrants, can create major shifts in an industry that challenge companies.

Changes in business system configuration

Up to this point we have discussed developments in each of the business system groups and some of the key drivers that can affect all players within the macro business system. The outcome of these developments might result in a different configuration of the business system in as much as some of the traditional players might disappear or new categories arise. Reconfiguration may take place in various forms. One particular group of industry participants might spawn a new group by splitting in two. Alternatively, a particular player group might disappear through elimination or combination of two industry stages. Finally, the entire industry is affected by moves to either forward or backward integrate.

Splitting of a given stage in the business system can happen when a new function suddenly appears and a group of independent companies begins to serve that new function. In the computer industry, the emergence of the personal computer spawned an entire new set of distributors/retailers selling PCs to companies and individual buyers. Before this event computers were sold directly through company-owned branch offices. The PC age thus resulted in a new class of industry players adding an additional stage in the PC industry business system.

Industry business system stages can sometimes be combined as one stage is absorbed into another. Essentially, one of the players in a business system takes over the function of another and, although the same functions are performed, the independent 'box' disappears. In many consumer goods industries we have seen the disappearance of independent wholesalers and their role has been absorbed by either consumer goods manufacturers or retail chain stores. For example, Carrefour in France or Aldi in Germany have both absorbed and replaced independent wholesalers.

The elimination of an industry stage usually occurs through technology as independent processes are combined into one new process. In the early 1980s a large number of jack-up oil-drilling rigs had to be towed from one drilling location to another, often over very large distances. The protruding legs of steel were pulled up for the trip. Very long steel legs had to be cut because having them protrude for more than 300 ft might result in the rig tipping over if it swayed too much in a storm. With the advent of special ships that obtained a higher level of stability, the drilling rigs could be transported with the full length of steel legs protruding, some up to 400 ft. The technology of stabilizing the transporting ship therefore eliminated the expensive operation of cutting the large steel legs and having to mount them back on at the drilling site. Such a cutting and reassembly operation would cost more than $1 million. The new ships eliminated this separate stage from the process (Jeannet, 1986).

Backward and forward integration tends to eliminate independent business system stages. However, the integration level does not often include an entire industry. In paint manufacturing, many paint companies are backwards integrated into resin manufacturing, an important raw material. However, there are still a large number of independent resin makers, or merchant resin companies, that sell resins on the open market. These companies mostly sell to smaller firms who are not backwards integrated and sell specialized resins to the larger paint companies. Both backward and forward integration therefore occurs side by side with separate business system stages. What are important in this analysis are the trends and the direction of events.

Developing an industry vision

Eventually, the analyst will be challenged to take the macro business system apart and understand how the individual pieces fit together. More importantly, managers will have to think about how an entire macro business system will be configured in the future. Since forward-looking business strategies depend on a view of how the industry will work, more and more firms will have to think harder about how their industry will look in the years to come. This process of anticipating the future industry within which to compete is properly termed 'developing an industry vision'.

Using concepts and terms developed by Porter, the evolution of a macro business system into the future could begin with an understanding of the five forces explained earlier (Porter, 1985). However, each of the separately identified stages of the business system is subject to the five forces, and the sum total of their impact on all players eventually leads to a new industry business system configuration. The configuration may include splitting, elimination or separation of various stages, as discussed above.

Tracking the drivers in the macro business system and understanding how each group of participants influences the participants in other stages requires an assessment of which stage in the business system has the most influence. The fundamental assessment to be made is to find the source of power, or the stage that can drive the others. This can best be described as redrawing the business system whereby each stage (or block) is drawn as a set of interlocking cogwheels. Once the wheels are engaged, the analysis will uncover the driving wheel or the crank for the system. The driving wheel in a structure will determine the speed and direction of all other wheels. The same is true in an industry. Understanding the location of the driving wheel and, even more importantly, anticipating changes where the driving wheel function is performed is one of the most important aspects of developing an industry vision.

Industry evolution

What most account managers need to be aware of are fundamental shifts in how an industry works, thus leading to changes in the driving wheel and the role of each of the other parts or industry stages. One well-considered approach is the development of industry scenarios (Porter,

1985). These shifts usually stem from a major change in the flow of the macro business system. Although we will see later that determining such shifts alone is not sufficient, it is nevertheless a first and significant step in developing a market advantage for a company.

The pharmaceutical industry acts as an example. We will describe possible shifts in the industry, but do not claim that our view will prevail.

The traditional pharmaceutical industry macro business system consisted of the raw material (chemical compound) suppliers used by pharmaceutical companies as a basis for their drugs. Pharmaceutical firms transformed these fine chemicals into drugs, developed and researched new drugs, tested their drugs and marketed those drugs through large salesforces to independent physicians or other healthcare organizations, depending on the health industry structure of a given country. This business system was characterized by the powerful role of integrated pharmaceutical firms that were the main drivers of the industry (Yoshino & Jeannet, 1995).

Present changes, both expected and apparent, in the pharmaceutical industry point towards a splitting up of roles hitherto performed by pharmaceutical firms, but in the future possibly performed by specialist companies. With the increased role of biotechnology, many specialist firms have evolved specializing in the drug-discovery process. These independent, small start-up firms then license their drugs to much larger pharmaceutical firms, which take them through the rest of the development cycle, including testing, and eventually market the product worldwide. If this trend continues, an entire new stage in the pharmaceutical business system would be created, one that up to now was always part of the pharmaceutical company stage.

Looking downstream towards marketing, the entire testing mechanism is being revolutionized by independent testing firms that can be hired by pharmaceutical firms to test the efficacy of their drugs. Usually these are tested in the market through hospitals and other research organizations. This means that another step in the value-creation process might become a separate stage in the business system. The end result is an evolution that leads us to draw the business system entirely differently for pharmaceuticals in the next decade.

The processes discussed in this chapter may seem rather imprecise to an analytical mind. We have entered the realm of industry vision. Our challenge is to envision how the industry business systems of which our companies are part will evolve. In this sense, we are becoming weather forecasters. We can compare this to forecasting the weather using a series of satellite photographs from outer space, looking down on a particular territory, tracking the evaluation of the clouds (if there are any) over time and consequently projecting the pattern into the near future.

The various building blocks of our macro business systems are continually updated to reflect the dynamics present in the industry. If we are to develop strategies that result in strong market advantage to our firms, we must look ahead and develop strategies for the industry that we are expected to meet in the future. We would fail if we developed account strategies for tomorrow on the basis of yesterday's dynamics of our industries. Recent research has shown that rapidly growing companies typically have a very clear and realistic vision of their industry and its expected course of evolution (Alahuhta, 1990).

CONCLUSION

Why do global account managers have to be concerned about macro and industry business systems? At the beginning of this chapter we made it clear that competitive analysis today includes far more than we saw in the past. Global account managers need to move beyond narrow direct competitive analysis (which Porter calls industry rivalry; Porter, 1985). Account managers must look further than what is normally called 'customers', who are often the firms that are one step downstream of the business system. The analysis must move all the way downstream, sometimes including multiple stages in the business system, to include all downstream industry participants. Equally, a proper perspective on the industry involves a look at any upstream participants of a firm's industry.

Analysing the Global Logic   4
of a Customer's Business

In the previous chapter we showed how a global account team can get close to a customer's business through an in-depth analysis of the customer's industry. In this chapter we would like to deal with the issue of globalization, an important element for account teams who understand their mandate as global. In particular, we would like to show how an account team can answer the question 'How global does our customer's strategy have to be?', as this greatly affects the account strategy.

Needless to say, we could also focus the same analytical approach on the company's own business. However, since we are trying to answer some underlying questions on the customer's business, this chapter is written from the perspective of a global account team attempting to understand the extent of the global pressure facing its client.

The same approach, if applied to the account team's own company, would also yield an interesting analysis of the required global response to customers. As a result, we have separately flagged that aspect since it provides us with guidance on the relevance of instituting a global account management structure.

Our analytical approach is based on an understanding of global logic as it applies to a customer's business. Under global logic we comprehend a strong pressure to provide a global response. An unattended strong global logic would lead to a negative competitive response on the part of the client company or, in other words, the client firm would suffer competitively in the event that it does not account for the strong global logic.

Our research over time has shown that there are several sources of global logic, and that it is paramount for a firm to understand each and come to terms with the relative strength stemming from all of these sources. We separate those global logics based on the customer's environment from those that are based on the industry and competitive environment. Consequently we describe each of the logics, beginning with those that are customer based.

CUSTOMER-BASED GLOBAL LOGICS

Global customer logic

Among customers globalization can occur at three different levels: customer need, customer benefit and product features. Each of these levels may return a different answer, and a manager with a global mindset needs to interpret the pattern of responses into a differentiated globalization strategy.

First, let's look at *customer needs*. On a generic level, we can investigate customers in different countries in a given category to understand if their underlying needs are similar or different. Notice that the term 'similar' is preferred over 'identical' or 'the same'. Similarity in the context of global customer analysis is more meaningful, and identical often connotes the term of an absolute. For example, the need for protection of wooden surfaces is probably global. Equally, the need for children to play is present everywhere. These simple examples indicate that paint (wood surface protection) or toys (child's play) are needs that face global customers. In our view, it would be appropriate to describe products satisfying worldwide needs as globalized on a need level. Many products face that test and the vast majority of companies have customers with global needs. This is not a very deep form of globalization and still leaves room for a considerable amount of difference at other levels.

Companies that face customers exhibiting global needs have a chance to capitalize on that, but their strategies will have to recognize this rather shallow level of globalization. It is the most common form and would not allow a firm to run a very integrated global strategy. Products that are aimed at customers with global needs can be called *global product categories*, as they are present, or needed, in most parts of the world. It is to be expected that they will differ extensively based on local factors, unless globalization goes beyond global needs.

The next layer of globalization might occur around the concept of *customer benefits*. Here, we ask the question: 'Are customers buying our products for the same reasons or with the same benefits in mind?' Even if we find ourselves in a global category, there is still ample room for the customer to purchase our products or services with different goals in mind and for different purposes.

Let's take a simple product such as bicycles. Purchased by customers around the globe and thus a global product category, they are a transportation vehicle in a country such as China and are purchased for the purpose of physical fitness in a country such as the US. Similar differences can be found with motorcycles, which are outselling cars in countries such as India and are used as the primary transportation means for someone who cannot purchase an automobile. In general fewer differences in benefits exist within industrial products, and the more we deal with high-technology products the more likely it is that the reason for the purchase and the use/intent are similar around the globe.

For a product classified as of global benefit, the marketing task on a global scale is different compared to classification only in the global product category. Customers exhibiting global benefit behaviour require a different strategy to those that are simply part of a global category but purchase for different reasons.

Finally, there is a third element of interest to potential global firms. The question turns from use and rationale for buying to focus on the particular features needed. For products where the features are largely identical around the world, such as 35 mm film, physical product standardization has a chance of succeeding. We can start to speak of *global products* where the features of the product are essentially the same around the world.

It is not difficult to find examples where the use conditions are such that differences in the environment dictate different product features. Standardized products are not common in the consumer goods industry, whereas the similarity tends to be much greater for technical products used under specific manufacturing conditions.

As we review our global customer logic, it is important to avoid the trap of asking the question 'Are you facing a global customer?' on a simplified basis and instead to distinguish between the various levels on which globalization might occur. We may face customers who consistently display the same general need (global category) but purchase the product or service for different reasons. Or we may have customers who want the same physical products (global product) but purchase them for different reasons in different countries. Several combinations exist. What is important is to differentiate the question and begin asking it in a different form. 'To what level is your customer global?' is often a more appropriate question than forcing the analysis into the binary global/non-global category.

The presence of significant global customer logic, particularly when benefits or features are very similar, dictates action on the part of the company. Ignoring strong global customer logic risks losing business. On the other hand, companies need to understand that if they market products as if there were strong customer logic, but in reality it is weak or not present, the risk becomes over-globalization and loss of attractiveness due to over-standardization. Finding the proper balance is a challenge for companies with global ambitions.

Any global account team analysing its customer's business needs to assess to what extent its customer faces a global customer logic. The extent of that logic and its pervasiveness drive a customer's global strategy in its industry.

Determining global purchasing logic

When looking at your customers' customers, not only what these customers want to purchase but how they buy counts. Here we are really asking the question: 'How do their customers buy their products?' We need to know if there is any global logic streaming from their customers' purchasing behaviour.

The analysis of global purchasing logic has its roots in the purchase range, or the distance that customers are likely to 'travel' to search for the best buy. Here we need to understand customers' purchasing behaviour. Several factors may be used as indicators for the presence of global market logic: distance or range of buying patterns, distribution or delivery arrangements and the phenomenon of grey markets. Each of these is described in detail below.

Global purchasing logic is present when customers search over a wider radius for their products or services. When such logic is completely absent, customers would only contract locally or nationally for purchases. In many industries today corporate purchasing is still restricted to national markets. At times local legislation fosters such practices. The local buyer does not search around the world for best bargains and is not likely to be influenced by competing offers in other countries. On the other hand, we speak of the presence of strong global market logic where customers scour the world for best bargains and are not reluctant to cover large distances to obtain the best deal for their firms.

Developments in the automotive industry offer an excellent example of this changing practice (*Financial Times*, 1993). Car assemblers purchase about half their cost base from outside component suppliers, some captive and others independent (Jeannet, 1993c). For decades, the purchasing pattern was to source such components from nearby suppliers, usually located in the same country or region. US companies tended to buy from US component suppliers, whereas European and Japanese firms formed their own. This created a myriad of smaller component firms with relatively small volumes. Once car assemblers became aware of the opportunity to save on costs through better purchasing, they increasingly purchased components from the most cost-effective firm, even if that firm was located on another continent.

This trend towards global sourcing, which extends the supply chain for the purchasing company beyond its country or region, has become a major factor affecting global market logic in the automotive industry. Other industries such as electronic components have shown similar patterns. Automotive component suppliers thus faced increased global market logic as a result of this development (*Wall Street Journal*, 1998).

The need to supply worldwide, with consistency but in separate locations, is another trend that is indicative of global purchasing logic. In many industries companies want their operations spread over the world supplied by a consistent supplier that can cover all plant locations. The purchasing strategy of these customers is for global purchasing contracts almost eliminating competitors that cannot be present in all locations.

In a recent example Groupe Schneider, a French-based firm with a major interest in the electrical power-distribution business, had acquired manufacturing operations in Europe and the US. Rather than operating the various businesses on an independent basis, Schneider realized that major production efficiencies might be realized if the company's production and sourcing strategies were integrated worldwide. As a result, Schneider approached several of its materials suppliers with a request to offer a package of products across all of its worldwide operations. Preferred suppliers were to be selected on the basis of long-term commitment to Schneider and global coverage. This request caught some suppliers by surprise when they realized that they did not have complete coverage of all the regions where Schneider operated (Jeannet, 1996b).

Professional service businesses also offer good examples of the effect of global purchasing logic. When selecting their statutory auditors, multinational firms exhibit strong preferences for auditing firms that can deliver an integrated audit, simultaneously, at their various locations around the world. This requires the audit firm to have its own global delivery system. Audit firms without such an international network are forced to join with other firms or be left out. This notion of a strong purchasing logic in their industry was one of the drivers for the rash of global mergers announced in autumn 1997, for example.

In all of these cases, clients, through their purchasing policies, exhibited strong global customer purchasing logic requiring suppliers to adapt their strategies or ignore them at their peril.

The previous section viewed customers largely on a business-to-business basis. However, many firms market through intermediaries, such as independent distributors, wholesalers or retailers. The purchasing characteristics of these intermediate channel members thus partially determine the extent of a global purchasing logic. In the past most of these intermediate channel members viewed their markets as local or regional. Typically, companies appointed country-specific distributors with exclusive territories. Wholesalers, to the extent that they played a role, were country specific. Most of all retailers, in their own operations, rarely spread across several countries. As a result, very low global retail or wholesale purchasing logic was traditionally exerted from this direction.

In many consumer markets, strong global consumer purchasing logic emanates from the 'travelling consumer'. With international travel continuing to experience substantial growth rates, the world is developing a group of discriminating consumers who require preferred services wherever they travel. Telephone services, for example, are a product that has had to respond to this emerging trend. With more people on the move, telephone operators not only offer mobile phones, but also new technology such as the GSM-type digital phones that allow consumers to buy a phone in one country and use it across Europe and Asia. Hotels, and even banking, as demonstrated by Citibank's global consumer services, are other examples of the travelling consumer looking for products and services everywhere (*Fortune*, 1993).

The emergence of *grey markets*, sometimes referred to as parallel imports, is a third indicator of global market logic. As most international firms have experienced, grey markets develop when price differentials between two countries become large enough that some other company or agent can engage in arbitrage and profit from the difference. Grey market behaviour has existed in the air ticket market, where consumers and executives alike have learned that the booking location determines prices, and thus where to book the best deals.

The grey market phenomenon exists for both consumer and industrial products and emerges particularly when two currencies move apart and prices begin to vary. What is important is the signalling effect of the emergence of grey markets. They indicate that customers do not only buy locally, but also react to offers from different parts of the world. Grey markets signal that global market logic, although dormant prior to the event, may in fact be present.

We currently live in a world where the purchasing range of companies and consumers alike is extended due to better information and its more rapid spread. As a result, many companies experience increasing global market logic, and this phenomenon has even appeared in industry sectors previously known for strictly local buying. Some of these changes are also driven by legislation, and the well-known efforts of the European Union as part of its Europe 1992 integrated market initiative contributed to push many sectors to more regional, even global market logic.

Global information logic

In previous sections we concentrated on how customers purchase (global purchasing logic) or what they actually desire (global customer logic). Recently we came across another type of logic that is different from the first two but also relates to the customer base, namely the information acquisition strategy of a company's customers. By information acquisition we mean the way customers scan the environment, the type of media they read or are exposed to, and to what extent they go to obtain information about products and services a long distance from home.

Traditional coverage of information acquisition is well documented in standard marketing textbooks (Kotler, 2002). Typically, consumers or business customers would scan the local media before making a particular purchasing decision. There was very little global information logic in the customer base that influenced international firms.

More recent developments, however, have made such influences more pervasive and thus affect the presence of global information logic. Many business-to-business customers in technology-driven sectors tend to read specific magazines or publications from mostly the United States, thus making that information available to buyers in other countries. A Japanese buyer, reviewing a US-based industry publication, thus acts to acquire information on a global scale, not merely locally. This is particularly true for such sectors as information technology, communications, computers and medical instruments, where the US is viewed as the lead market and developments there are quickly spotted elsewhere.

As a next step, buyers might go to specific trade shows with a global following. Such shows exist in both the US and Europe, and for some industries they are the most important events. For example telecoms has a major show taking place every four years in Geneva, Switzerland. Visitors come from all over the world, thus creating a global information-acquisition opportunity. Other important trade shows can be identified for many specific industries.

Business executives' ever more frequent travel exposes many buyers to information outside their home country. To the extent that they follow up and actively pursue such information, global information logic exists.

Possibly the most important change in information acquisition is the development of the Internet and the World Wide Web (WWW). This electronic tool, which is taking the world by storm, is rapidly becoming a new mode of looking for product or service information. Consumers anywhere can go on to the Web and locate product information in a different country, thus creating strong global information logic. In fact, it is even influencing global purchasing logic to the extent that actual product purchases are becoming more common.

Any company seeking to gain a thorough understanding of the forces that shape the global marketplace must recognize the changing ways in which customers acquire information. Neglecting global information logic in a business would put the company's entire communications strategy at risk. Any global strategy needs to be based on a thorough understanding of this logic.

Give background to logic based in industry environment

When the debate on the merits of globalization began in the early 1980s, the predominant assumption among proponents of globalization was the belief that consumers or customers were becoming more similar, thus driving the trend towards globalization. This chapter is largely devoted to these trends and has explained in detail the sources of the various pressures that might compel firms to adopt some form of global strategy. However, there are still many firms where pressure from the customer base itself is not sufficiently strong to warrant all-out global strategies. As our experience with countless firms has shown, other forces, often related to an industry's competitive behaviour or inherent economics, may outshine customer-based forces as a source of globalization. These industry-based global logics were discussed in Chapter 3.

Global customer logic, global purchasing logic and global information logic all focus on customers: what they want, how they purchase or how they search for information. The next generic global logics focus on the industry, either on competition, industry structure, KSFs, critical mass, or regulations. Clearly, these forces on companies to globalize are different from customer derived pressures.

INDUSTRY-BASED GLOBAL LOGICS

Global competitive logic

Competition is a potent force driving globalization. When competition generates a compelling argument to pursue globalization, we speak of a global competitive logic. The principal question to ask in assessing competitive logic is: 'Are we meeting the same competitors around the world?' In some industries a company might be present in many markets but always find a different set of competitors, indicating low global competitive logic. In other industries – and this is increasingly the case – companies run into the same competitors wherever they go. Particularly where industrial products are concerned, only a handful of firms compete everywhere and global players always encounter the same firms. When a company faces the same players worldwide, a good argument for global competitive logic can be made.

Over time, we have also learned that the presence of competitors is not the only indicator to watch. Even more telling is whether the company encounters the same strategy. This would signal more coordinated competition and enhance the need to respond. In some sectors, global competitive logic is so strong that it may overtake other global logic dimensions and become an end in itself. Several examples exist where global competition is reduced to two major players, staking out territory in chess-like fashion. The experiences in soft drinks (Coca-Cola vs Pepsi-Cola), photographic film (Kodak vs Fuji) or construction machinery (Caterpillar vs Komatsu) are typical examples of such global competitive constellations (Allen, 1992).

Global competitive logic develops along a vector ranging from a strictly national competitive pattern, where firms compete nationally and different sets of firms compete in different countries, all the way to the pure global competitive form, where very few firms compete everywhere. It is therefore helpful to look at competition in the form of different theatres. Country-specific theatres imply that a firm's competitive situation is determined country by country, and that a competitive situation in one country is independent of that in another country. In this case each market requires a new and different game with a separate starting gate. This type of local-for-local competition is still prevalent (but no longer exclusively) in service industries, retailing, contracting and small artisan shops. Here, little can be leveraged from one market to another and a firm's competitive strength is not enhanced by positions built elsewhere. Competitive strength can be measured in terms of local market share only.

In some industries the relevant competitive theatre may be regional, with different players in Europe, North America and Asia/Pacific. Regional competitive theatres are characterized by a lack of competitive synergy across regions, i.e. global, as competitive positions cannot be leveraged into other regions. Competitiveness could be measured in regional market share, whereby local shares would be less important than the regional share. Conversely, the global competitive theatre is characterized by the capability of all competitors to reach into one another's home territory, thus eliminating carefully coveted 'sanctuaries' or protected markets. When a global competitive theatre applies, competitive position is not simply the addition of various local strengths. We can now think in terms of global market share to measure competitiveness, and local or even regional share as less indicative of competitive strength.

In today's rapidly changing environment, industries can quickly migrate from one type of theatre to another. The white goods industry serves as an excellent example (Allen, 1990). In the early 1980s the white goods industry structure in Europe was characterized by 70 or more players, most of them locked into small, country-specific markets. In the US there were a few large players (GE, Whirlpool, Maytag, White-Westinghouse) and a similar structure existed in Japan. Clearly the relevant theatre was regional, but in Europe one could even speak of country-specific theatres. When Electrolux concluded that for cost reasons it needed to break out of what was largely a regional market in Nordic Europe, major acquisitions were made throughout Europe and in the US (White-Westinghouse) (Lorenz, 1989). Thus moving towards the view of a global theatre, this prompted major moves on the part of many key players. GE, up to that time the largest company, became quickly affiliated with other European firms. Whirlpool acquired the Philips appliance business and became the largest player in Europe, moving Electrolux to second place and GE to third. Within a short period the dynamics of the market had changed from national to regional, and then to a global theatre (*BusinessWeek*, 1987).

Companies need to keep in mind the dangers of ignoring significant global competitive logic. When such logic exists, they are well advised to keep competitive viewpoints in mind when embarking on a decision on whether to adopt a global strategy, or which global strategy to adopt. Obtaining a clear view of the type of competitive logic involved is thus a prerequisite for forming an appropriate strategy.

Global industry logic

While the presence or absence of global competitive pressure is relatively easy to spot, global industry logic is one of those forces that are not easily visible, and we often labelled it 'non-visible' globalization. The question we need to answer is: 'Are we competing in a global industry?' Remember, we have already dealt with competition separately, so the unit of analysis consists of the nature of the value chain, the overall structure of the industry and the relevant key success factors (KSF), as discussed in Chapter 3.

It may be easier to think of the set of KSFs required in an industry as an industry code, as already indicated (Jeannet, 1996a). Most companies crack this code for their home markets. Firms expend great effort to crack the relevant industry code, measured in terms of expertise, time, skills and investments. Once the code of an industry is cracked and the road to success lies open, companies have to ask whether the same code applies to another country, region or even the world. An industry with a global code is characterized by a similar set of KSFs governing success in that industry. Understanding that, a company can leverage this into other areas, thus obtaining more 'bang for the buck'.

Industries where the same set of KSFs applies worldwide are thus said to experience a greater amount of global industry logic. Conversely, industries where the KSFs differ substantially from country to country can be said to experience very little global industry logic. The implications of global industry logic are important for the development of global strategies. Having successfully navigated the code for an industry with worldwide application, a company has an incentive to take that experience elsewhere and obtain additional return on a lesson already learned. This reduces the cost of the original lesson, or 'code-cracking' experience.

Even when they understand the basic concept of industry codes, KSFs and the need to ask the question 'Does this code apply to one country alone, or are the codes essentially the same around the world?', managers will find that few industries exist where we can answer this in absolute terms. Global industry logic is not just black and white, it comes in gray or intervals, so managers must assess the degree of global or local for each industry. For some industries it may be helpful to draw some simple graphs to illustrate the concept.

Let's use the paint industry as an example (Jeannet, 1993a). There are a number of dimensions along which the industry can be segmented: geographically, by application industry (automotive, marine and decorative) and by technology (water borne, solvent based, powder). For a company such as ICI Paints, which runs paint operations around the world, would the KSFs encountered by each regional or country organization be similar (Jeannet, 1993b)? Although there is a need to adjust paint to the local operating environment (climate, substrata), paint operations *per se* might be considered largely similar. On the other hand, significant differences may exist in the various application segments. The automotive industry, with its particular needs and its globalizing customer base, experiences a high degree of uniformity, suggesting that automotive OEM paint operations can be run with a high degree of similarity, thus the relevant code to crack that segment is likely to be very similar around the world. On the other hand in decorative paint, an industry that still differs substantially from country to country and in which most paint moves through the retail sector, the relevant segment code might be more different than similar.

The paint industry example illustrates the need to look not only at the industry but also at the relevant sub-segments, and to ask questions regarding similarity of codes on several levels. In most instances, as companies go through such an exercise they will find that the important judgement to be made is an assessment of how different or similar the industry is. Once similarities have been identified, however shallow, the next step requires the company to take advantage of these similarities in codes through leverage. Since global leverage is one of those terms frequently used but often applied in a cavalier fashion, it is important to look at leverage in more specific terms to see how this might apply in the context of global industry logic.

Leverage means that we gain additional effectiveness from doing something a second time, or we might be able to do it better by spreading it over more business volume. The first type of leverage comes from applying lessons from one part of the world to another. This can be seen as similar to tuition, the educational fees to be paid for attending university. If a company wants to obtain such leverage through its global network of companies, it must provide for a process by which the lessons, and the related cost for learning them, are paid for only once and others learn from them. This is much easier said than done, as we have seen earlier with the not-invented-here (NIH) syndrome, and requires managers who can evaluate lessons for their applicability regardless of their home base or experience base. Many opportunities to gain leverage under global industry logic are thus under-utilized, and many global firms resemble classrooms where many students attend, all paying high tuition, but it is not clear whether anyone is learning the lessons taught.

The second form of leverage, namely sharing resources to do something better, is also difficult to achieve. If all local units of a worldwide operating firm were left on their own, there would be a substantial duplication of resources. A firm applying this strategy well would gain additional competitiveness.

One example of this type of leverage is Electrolux, the Sweden-based white goods manufacturer that transformed industry competition through its assessment of KSFs. Electrolux concluded that while customer requirements differ from country to country, each of its appliances nevertheless had a substantial number of components 'under the hood' that were identical. Leverage thus came from building volume in these same components or sharing them across a diverse line of products, thus gaining efficiency (*Business International*, 1986).

Global size logic

Related to global industry logic is global size logic. Often referred to as the need to build critical mass, global size logic is an important driver in the global strategies pursued by many firms. In many industries a minimal size of a key activity is needed to compete effectively. In some ways it is part of a KSF or industry code. The presence of any form of critical mass clearly relates to globalization, because strong global size logic typically forces companies to adjust by spreading market coverage to gain the required minimum size. In many industries, the presence of global size logic even means that no single market can pay off the fixed investments required to enter.

Companies need to search for global size logic by finding out if anywhere in their business some steps, departments or functions exist that would be inefficient below such a critical mass. Some of the easiest examples to understand stem from the pharmaceutical industry. For pharma companies, the average cost required to bring a new drug from molecule development to market introduction is about $800 million (*Medical Advertising News*, 2002). Given that a pharmaceutical company cannot spend an unlimited amount on research, this minimum fixed investment needs to be amortized within the research budget (15–20 per cent of sales). In addition, patent filing early in the molecule-development stage and long lead times for market introduction mean that effective time in the market is cut to about ten years. If the drug is to earn sufficient profits, the pharmaceutical company needs to obtain sales of about $1.2–1.5 billion over the product lifetime, or $120–150 million per year. Therefore, it needs to be active in many markets to obtain such volumes.

Merger activity in the pharmaceutical industry has clearly been driven by global size logic strongly perceived by many of these players. In the early phase of consolidation, the mergers were between a large acquirer and smaller firms who had become marginalized by strong global size logic. Glaxo's acquisition of Wellcome fits into this category. Other mergers took place between mid-size firms in an effort to leapfrog into the big league. The Pharmacia/Upjohn combination would be part of this trend. Finally, the latest trend has been the mega-merger between members already part of the big league: Ciba-Geigy merging with Sandoz to form Novartis, thus coming close to global leadership in pharmaceuticals, and the merger between Glaxo and SmithKline Beecham to form GlaxoSmithKline are two of the earlier examples. A more recent example of a mega-merger is represented by the absorption of both Warner-Lambert and Pharmacia/Upjohn into Pfizer, propelling the latter into a position of global leadership in terms of volume and market share (Class, 2002).

In the financial sector we have witnessed major mergers between large companies. Among financial institutions in Europe, Union Bank of Switzerland and Swiss Bank Corporation merged to form United Bank of Switzerland (UBS), becoming the largest European bank and one of the largest in the world (*Financial Times*, 1998). This merger was caused by a perceived need to gain more critical mass in the investment banking area, which requires a considerable amount of capital. The two banks were already among the leaders in private banking, commercial banking and domestic retail banking. The combination of Zurich Insurance of Switzerland with the financial services arm of the UK's BAT was a major merger in the insurance sector. This combination created a more global coverage in insurance and fund management, where both firms strive to achieve sufficient size to compete globally.

Minimum size pointing to the presence of global size logic may exist in different parts of a firm's operations. For an airline it may be in the worldwide reservation system. For other companies this critical mass may be dictated by high fixed costs in a logistic system, a required sales presence or other elements. What is needed is to understand the business system and the industry of a company well enough to ferret these parts out, identify them and be clear on the strength of the size logic. As more and more firms face an increasing amount of fixed expenditure, particularly in the R&D area, many firms find themselves pushed into a new game through increasing global size logic.

The need to achieve critical mass on a global scale has created a substantial momentum towards mergers that improve both the global ranking of a firm and the global size of a business. We can expect many more of these mergers in the future.

Global regulatory logic

The regulatory environment is one of the most important elements for some industries. This is true for healthcare, but also for industries such as banking, insurance, airlines, telecommunications and much of the new media. Global regulatory logic exists when a company would face a need to extend itself globally due to different regulatory forces, or face competitive disadvantage by not doing so.

Looking at the healthcare industry helps illustrate the concept. Regulatory affairs, such as for pharmaceuticals or medical implants, are still dominated by country-specific regulatory bodies. For the United States this is the Federal Food and Drug Administration (FDA). Some of the regulations or permissions granted to market a drug in the US at times differ from those in other countries. In general, regulatory practice in the US has been accused of being slower than in Europe. Because the time period between patent granting and market entry is important in determining the economic success of a new product, companies planning to operate in the US alone would be limited to exploiting new products, compared to others able to launch earlier or simultaneously in Europe or other markets.

This presence of global regulatory logic would therefore require the company to have a launching pad in more than one area of the world and, in particular, in those countries where approval might be gained first. Ares-Serono, a Swiss-based biotechnology firm with a global leadership position in fertility drugs, was the first company to seize on the opportunity to apply for approval under the new European regulatory arrangement. The new body, the European Medicines

Evaluation Agency (EMEA), approved Serostim, a growth hormone developed by the company to fight wasting due to AIDS.

In the production of many drugs, the US-based FDA has become the *de facto* standard for manufacturing processes. The FDA good manufacturing process (GMP) approval is necessary for any plant shipping drug products into the US. Since it is increasingly impossible to dedicate factories to individual markets, the globally or regionally focused factory must be able to master GMP to ship to the US. A manufacturing base for a firm in Europe exporting to the US market thus becomes subject to GMP approval. When building a plant, or designing a new manufacturing process, GMP has to be factored in from the outset. This tends to level the playing field for more firms, albeit at a higher level, thus increasing the global regulatory logic. Once this most difficult regulatory hurdle is overcome, a company might as well ship worldwide because it has cleared the hurdles for many other countries as well.

In the telecommunications industry, traditional standards for telephone signalling, equipment and network systems were nationally configured. This was also true for cellular networks. As a result, a cellular customer in Finland, for example, could not use the phone when traveling to France or to the United States. The move to newer standards, in particular the GMS standard pioneered by European telephone carriers, meant that customers could begin to use their phones wherever they travelled. Rather than finding regional or local standards, the world is rapidly moving to the adoption of one standard. This creates strong global regulatory logic and makes it possible for manufacturers to market their equipment across multiple markets. The rapid growth of Ericsson and Nokia in mobile telecommunications networks in the US is a result of these changes.

The financial services sector is another area where standards or regulations were typically national. Through both the World Trade Organization and the integration movement in the European Union, regulatory affairs have become more closely coordinated. As local barriers disappear or are reduced, global regulatory logic makes it possible for players to cross borders. This is one reason that we have witnessed cross-border mergers in insurance (Allianz, Axa, Zurich Insurance), banking (ING and Barings) and the many acquisitions of financial institutions on a global scale (*Financial Times*, 1998).

Global regulatory logic is therefore low where there are significant differences in regulatory behaviour and high where approval or regulatory practices are similar. The past decade has seen enormous shifts in how national or local governments regulate industries. The result has been an overall reduction in regulatory barriers, and a general increase in global regulatory logic, which affects the competitive behaviour of firms active in previously highly regulated sectors.

ASSESSING PATTERNS OF GLOBAL LOGIC

The previous sections have concentrated on providing companies with an approach to probe for the intensity of the global logic in different parts of their business. Following that analysis, a company would have an appropriate reading of each of the chosen global logic dimensions. This section is devoted to converting these separate global logic readings on each dimension into a meaningful pattern for guiding global strategy. To accomplish this, the use of the 'spiderweb' is suggested. We will also discuss approaches to ensure that global logic analysis is performed in a sufficiently forward-looking manner so that future trends can be incorporated.

Selection of generic global logic dimensions

The global logics described above are generic dimensions, or global logics that occur in most industries we have reviewed. There is a tendency for these generic global logic dimensions to be seen as the only possible ones. This would be far from reality. While they are typically present in most industries, we suggest that each industry be separately analysed and that there may well be other dimensions more relevant for further analysis. Some creativity is thus required and business teams facing a thorough analysis of the relevant global logic present in their industry are well advised to use a measure of judgement in applying generic dimensions in a 'cookie-cutter' approach.

Our experience with the creation of the global logic concept might also be of value to aspiring globalists elsewhere. Originally we recognized only four generic global logic dimensions. As our analytical experience grew, however, additional dimensions emerged. It is to be expected that over time additional generic global logic dimensions may be uncovered, possibly even before this book goes to print.

Aside from the more generic global logic dimensions, experience also shows that some generic global logics are in reality a composite of several related logics, forming broader rays or vectors. As we have seen, global purchasing logic can be measured at the level of business to business, the individual consumer, or retail, wholesale or distribution, thus combining to form a vector with several dimensions. The global purchasing logic may not be of equal intensity along all of these dimensions. Consequently, any analyst must be careful to understand the depth and breadth of these vectors before committing to a detailed analysis.

Measuring global logic intensity (via ordinal measurements)

Rather than reducing global intensity to a single denominator or measurement, we suggest an approach that might accept different measurements along different global logic dimensions. To achieve this, we will have to reduce the various global logic dimensions to some comparable measurement.

After diligently performing a global logic analysis, a company may be facing a considerable amount of data or experience that, on its own, is not yet comparable across the various different dimensions. Some care must now be taken to convert the analysis into more standardized measures. The rationale for using measurements stems from our experience that the forces for globalization, as captured through global logics, are not equally spread throughout the

Global logic dimensions	Ratings 1	2	3	4	5	6	7	8	9	10
Customer logic										
Purchasing logic										
Information logic										
Competitive logic										
Industry logic										
Size logic										
Regulatory logic										

Figure 4.1 Global logic ratings

business environment of a firm. To isolate the sources of strongest global logic, the analyst has the choice of two principle types of measurements: we can either measure in absolute terms or in ordinal/rank-order ratings.

Working with absolute measurements, we would have to convert each of the identified global logic dimensions into measurements, such as a rating along an index of 1–10, as shown in Figure 4.1, or 1–100. This would be a judgement based on global management experience by a company, business team or experienced executive.

Although convenient and easily implemented, the use of absolute ratings is to be discouraged for two reasons. First, it gives a semblance of precision that is simply not present in the real world, where the situation is much more complex. Although managers are quite used to making judgements about environmental conditions, experience has shown that on many scales they might have difficulty separating the global intensity across the various global logic dimensions. As we will see later, it does not serve a useful purpose if the dimensions are all rated 'highly global' or are all given ten out of

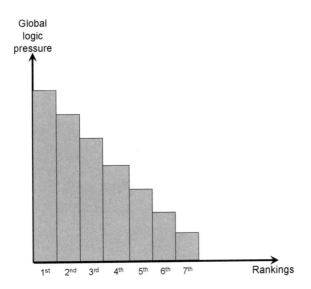

Figure 4.2 Global logic rankings

ten. In cases where all the global logic dimensions are highly global it requires further discussion to rank order these findings.

Measuring global logic using rank order

Since it will be of great importance to a company to understand the relative pressures emanating from the various global logics, we are much better served if we look for relevant or comparative rankings. Such comparative rankings allow us to rank-order the global logic intensity of each of the selected dimensions. Ranking would require a business team to agree which of the dimensions experiences the highest global logic pressure, which the second and so on, as shown in Figure 4.2.

ASSEMBLING GLOBAL LOGICS INTO MEANINGFUL PATTERNS

How, then, are we to conceptualize the various global logic measurements into a coherent pattern that will help companies appreciate the global pressures in their industries? When searching for appropriate ways to depict the complexity of global logics in

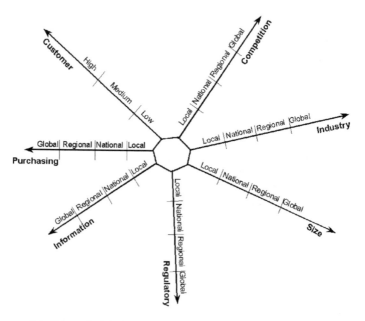

Figure 4.3 General global logic spiderweb chart

different industries, we discarded traditional histograms, bar charts and other composite measures. Instead, we adopted the 'spiderweb' chart so often used in business and economics journals.

Depicting the generic global logic dimensions starting in the centre of the chart, we can indicate extensive global pressure by the relative distance from the centre. A sample of a spiderweb is shown in Figure 4.3. A company facing an industry with little or even zero global pressure would show a small footprint. A company exposed to extensive global pressure would show a large, extensive footprint. Figure 4.4 contrasts a small-footprint spiderweb with a large-footprint spiderweb.

Categorizing generic global spiderwebs

For a complete and meaningful analysis, it is not sufficient to denote the size of the footprint alone. It makes a real difference to know the actual source of the dominating global pressure, thus forcing companies to identify the extreme ends of their spiderwebs.

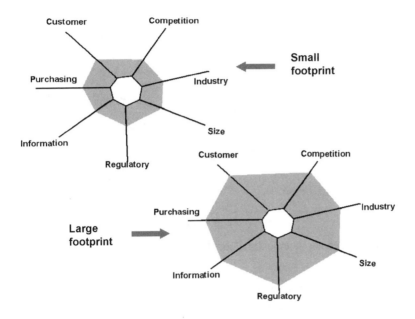

Figure 4.4 Global logic footprints

As we pointed out in Chapter 3, the initial debate surrounding globalization centred on markets and customers showing increasingly converging patterns of consumption. This 'Levitt' argument (Levitt, 1983), if translated into our conceptualization, would indicate that global pressures would primarily emanate from the consumer side, or global customer, purchase, or information logic. With a view that globalization was primarily driven by customers, the typical spiderweb chart would be heavily weighted in favour of customer sensitivity dimensions, as shown in Figure 4.5.

Experience indicates, however, that the measurements of global logic differ by industry. We found that customer-based global logics were not always the strongest. In many sectors, industry-based global logics (industry, competitive, size, regulatory) are relatively more pronounced and often outrank customer-based global logics. Industry-based logics are strong in those industries where significant differences exist among the global customer base but where the realities

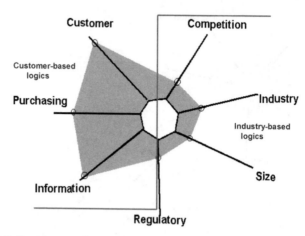

Figure 4.5 Customer vs industry global logic patterns

of competition and industry economics dictate a non-domestic approach. Typical examples of such industries would be cement, forestry, chemicals and other basic industries.

Visible vs invisible globalization

Different patterns do exist and we can only point out some of the generic ones. The dimensions, although sometimes correlated, can in fact describe different orthogonal patterns that frequently act independently of each other.

From experience of working with various firms operating in many industry environments, we have observed that the ratings for the chosen generic global logics are usually different. The chance of running a business where all elements show exactly the same global intensity is small. Rather, the intensity differs by global logic and the patterns exhibited by most firms will differ according to the industry they are in. However, given the fact that we are measuring the global intensity of an industry, not firms operating in the same competitive industry, the environment is expected to face an identical pattern of global logic.

Treating the various global logics as partly independent, or orthogonal, is based on the observation that companies face radically different globalization patterns in different industries. In some industries the external factors, such as global customer logic or global purchasing logic, may put greater pressure to globalize on a business. In other situations companies face largely hidden or industry-based global logic factors leading to globalization, in spite of differentiation forces among the customer base. In our experience global logic stemming from industry factors is more important and relevant for many industries than is that from customers or markets. This is particularly the case for some of the more technologically oriented industries and for many business-to-business situations.

Having a clear idea of the relevant spiderweb is a precondition for engaging in an articulate and informed globalization debate in any business or company. Managers should be aware that the spiderweb is highly industry specific, and in some instances even segment specific. How the output of the spiderweb analysis may be used to chart an actual globalization strategy will be the main point of the following chapter.

Global logic trends over time

Careful analysis of the relevant dimensions or logics of globalization should also lead to an understanding of the present and future state of an industry. We might be able to paint an accurate picture through an in-depth spiderweb analysis for a company at a moment in time, but there are forces at work that cause patterns to change. Typically, the forces at work in our rapidly globalizing economy tend to enhance the global logic working on firms. In some instances the changes can come about rather quickly, as we have seen in the case of global competitive logic where a move by one player can make all the others change their strategy.

In the major home appliance or white goods industry, the impetus given by Electrolux led to similar global strategies by Whirlpool, Maytag and GE. In the end, when Electrolux's original industry vision became reality, it was difficult to tell if this was as a result of a solid strategy or simply because all the players followed suit and thus realized the vision.

Outward moves on the spiderweb chart have been most prevalent in the areas of purchasing logic and competitive logic. On both dimensions we have witnessed considerable changes in business practices that have had more effect on global logic than in other areas. Customers have changed and will continue to change their requirements. However, movements along customer logic take more time and move more deliberately, and changes are often only noticeable over a longer period. In the areas of purchasing and competition, a single move by an important customer, or a major competitor's acquisition strategy, can throw an entire industry into globalization turmoil, effectively changing the overall global logic within a short time.

Equally, we should consider it possible for global logic forces to diminish along a given dimension. Although all of our examples have pointed in the direction of outward or increasing global pressure, we should not eliminate the possibility that global logic pressure might diminish across a given dimension as a result of different industry environments.

Anticipating global logic changes

Having noted that companies need to understand the future global spiderweb as a basis for their forward strategies, we should explore how such forward predictions can be made with some sense of authority. For that purpose, we suggest that the particular relationship of the various global logic dimensions can be an indicator of imminent changes.

One indicator could be a relatively high degree of global industry logic combined with low competitive logic. This would signal that while substantial opportunities for global logic exist, the industry itself has not yet stepped up its effort and is not conducting itself sufficiently globally. In this situation it would take only one major industry player to move everyone into a global game, much along the situation we have seen in white goods with Electrolux, or the airline industry based on early alliance moves by British Airways. When the competition is under-globalized compared to the global opportunity, competitive reaction is likely to occur that will change the nature of the competitive game.

Another dimension to watch out for is global purchasing logic. As we explained, this captures the purchasing behaviour of customers in the industry. To the extent that they are acting ahead of industry competitors (their suppliers in this case), a signal is sent to all industry participants that they themselves are not taking advantage of the full global imperative.

Finally, changes in the industry that lead to a substantial change in the global industry logic or critical mass logic are powerful indicators that further globalization will follow. Such a change might include the result of technological breakthroughs leading to a higher critical mass requirement, which in turn leads to greater volume needs driving companies into multiple markets.

The appropriate spiderweb analysis will thus include both a present and future type of analysis, combined with a future trend picture. Since changes in a firm's global logic pressure are very important and take time to internalize, companies are well advised to make their plans based on the future, not past or present global logic pressure.

Single vs multiple spiderwebs

An issue that frequently arises when examining global logic is the unit of analysis. As we pointed out earlier, global logic is inherent to an industry and is not company specific. However, some industries are very broad and are made up of a number of sectors or segments. When the global logic is reviewed, companies will need to be sensitive to any differences by segment or sector. In essence, the question of the number of logics needs to be taken into account. For industries with multiple sets of KSFs (key success factors), experience indicates that a different set of global logics might apply to each segment.

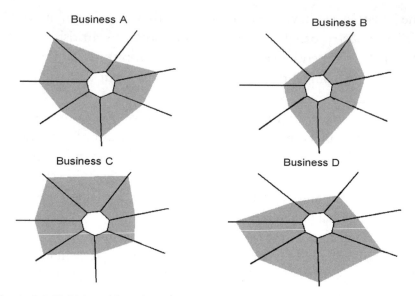

Figure 4.6 Multiple spiderweb patterns

The presence of multiple global logic spiderwebs for different business units, as shown in Figure 4.6, is a challenge for most companies. As we will outline in the next section, there is a direct relationship between the chosen generic global strategy and the particular spiderweb global logic pattern identified for an industry. If multiple patterns exist, multiple generic global strategies will have to be accommodated in parallel. This is a major source of challenges for multi-product or multi-segment companies as they globalize.

Actual industry vs perceived company global logic patterns

We have stressed that global logic measures the pressure present in a firm's industry. In that sense, the global logic spiderweb would be identical for all directly competing firms. All competitors would need to accommodate the global logic pressure. However, we can also depict the situation within a firm by judging the extent to which the global logic pressure is being followed. Each company operates on a certain view of the global market. Rather than probing for the factual

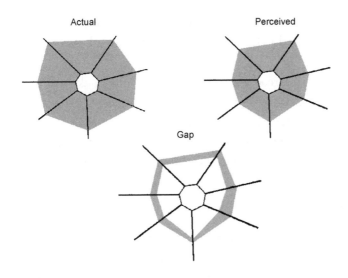

Actual   Perceived

Gap

Figure 4.7 Actual vs perceived global logic patterns

view or true state of the global logic pressure within a given industry, we can draw a pattern of how a particular firm is acting. This would tell us to what extent the company is operating on an over- or under-globalized view. Companies with a perception of less global logic than objectively identified would be operating in a state of under-globalization. The opposite would be true for firms who perceive the industry to have a higher global logic than objectively validated. Checking perceived against actual global logic can serve as a strong indicator of a company's globalization gap, as illustrated in Figure 4.7.

IMPLICATIONS FOR GLOBAL STRATEGIES

Throughout this chapter we have emphasized the role of global logic analysis. This type of diagnostic will become the centrepiece of the following chapters, where we will build extensively on those spiderwebs. Because of their central importance in understanding globalization and the global imperative for any firm, it is necessary again to caution readers in their application. All too often companies and executives tend to take a tool and apply it without care and insight, filling in the blanks in the same way one would fill out a mere form letter.

We hope that the reader has gained sufficient background on this analysis to appreciate that it must be conducted with considerable thought and requires the application of deep industry experience. Only then can we be confident that the output of the analysis will be of sufficient quality to base further global strategies on it.

CONCLUSION

This chapter has dealt with appropriate measurements for global logics and the type of interpretation or strategy implications that stem from these. We hope that it will serve as a stimulant for global account managers to approach their analytical tasks in a constructive and critical-thinking way, thus avoiding approaches that turn out to be mechanistic.

Understanding the Client's Strategy

5

In the previous two chapters we explained the industry structure and dynamics, as well as the relevant global logics. We can now focus our attention on a specific global key account. The process outlined in this chapter deals with appreciating the global key account's requirements and strategy, followed by establishing a link that will connect the company's sales team to the particular strategic requirements of the key account. The process is based on an understanding that successful global account teams need to make their accounts more successful in meeting industry requirements, thus forcing the team to demonstrate that it can in fact make the client or account more successful. The emphasis we are advocating is based on helping the global account meet its own KSFs in its specific industry, as analysed and outlined in the previous chapters.

ASSESSING THE ACCOUNT'S CORPORATE STRATEGY

The global account may be operating as a single business only. However, in many circumstances the global account team may deal with a division or strategic business unit (SBU) of a larger parent company. For this reason, we will separate the corporate from the business assessment.

At the corporate level, the account team needs to determine if there is a corporate strategy that deals with an entire business portfolio, covering a range of products. If so, the role of the target business unit as part of the entire portfolio needs to be understood. Comprehending the overall corporate strategy is important because it often sets the tone for all of the businesses, and the account team needs to be aware of this corporate reality if it is dealing with only part of the company, or a single division or business unit.

Monitoring ownership realities

Given today's financial markets, the account team will have to assess the ownership views of the client corporation. This means reviewing investment analysts' reports on performance, pressure on share price, shareholder value issues, quality of management, perceived potential and other related issues.

Every company is affected by the particular realities of ownership, although they tend to differ between public and privately held firms. Public firms are under substantial performance pressure in many industries and corporate strategy is adapted to respond to such pressures. In particular, the team needs to know if there are any businesses that might be spun off or sold and, if so, whether this applies to those parts of the company where the team intends to create a global account management relationship. An astute global key account team will be able to appreciate the corporate ownership realities and assess the potential impact on the business targeted for a global key account relationship.

The pressures affecting privately held firms are usually different. Although private firms do not depend on stock-market fluctuations, they are still in need of financing. Meeting cash-flow requirements is typically more important to these firms as they have less access to financing.

Finally, with divestments or spin-offs of divisions becoming a daily reality, global key account teams must always position themselves for that eventuality. When dealing with firms where this is a risk, anchoring the relationship in the appropriate unit or division will be of special importance.

The inverse can be true as well. If the global account team finds itself in a situation where the target client becomes involved in a merger, it needs to be positioned so that it could fend off any potential competitive suppliers with strong relationships from the newly acquired part. Consequently, monitoring the corporate realities of the client firm requires the global account team continually to envision future moves and prepare for the eventual sale, spin-off or acquisition of its 'relationship' by another firm, placing it at risk.

Understanding the financial footprint

A firm's financial footprint concerns its financial realities, its cash flow and its funds-flow cycle. The rate of sustainable growth needs to be understood. What does it take to support the business (assets, liabilities etc.)? How does the company measure its performance? Which financial yardstick should the company use?

In addition to assessing the corporate ownership and external view of a client, understanding the financial footprint is becoming very important. By financial footprint we mean more than merely the balance sheet or income statement as published in a company's annual report. It will be important for the account team to understand how the financial flows work through the company. Although myriad ratios may be tracked, here is a list of items that should appear on any global account team's shortlist:

- *Cash flow*. The client firm's cash flow is outlined in its published annual reports. The team needs to understand the impact of the cash-flow situation and how it relates to investors' expectations and comparisons to other, competing firms. Many firms also look at so-called operating free cash flow (OpFCF) to assess the future value of a firm. The information should be interpreted to indicate if the client company has sufficient cash flow to meet all of its strategic requirements. An important shortcoming of this analysis is the fact that most detailed financial information is available for the corporation only, and not for the target business or unit.
- *Profitability measures*. As we all know, profitability can be measured at different levels. Clearly, the account team needs to be familiar with the more standard measurements, such as income as a percentage of

sales and net profit against assets (ROI, RONA, ROCE, EBITDA, EBIT, margins etc.). As a prime source of this information, we suggest a review of investment analysts' reports. Despite the recently published shortcomings of these, the financial information displayed is often very detailed and needs to be separated from any type of investment recommendation. Furthermore, privately held firms are less likely to publish detailed figures, therefore profitability needs to be estimated through other means. The account team should be able to benchmark its target firm against competitors, so that it will be familiar with any business pressures emanating from insufficient profitability.

- *Asset intensity.* Any business will require a certain amount of financial assets to support its volume. Assets can be both liquid, such as working capital, or can be in the form of fixed assets, such as manufacturing plants. Under working capital we include inventories and accounts receivable, as well as cash needed to conduct the business. Since asset intensity is also a matter of choice depending on the degree of integration or outsourcing that a firm desires in its operations, relevant measures are likely to differ across different competitors. The account team needs to be familiar with the drivers of asset intensity and how its selected target company compares with what is required. Under-performance often triggers major actions such as closing plants, redundancies or sale of assets by management. More importantly, the account team may have a business proposition for its target client that may substantially enhance or improve the asset intensity, which could be important for a firm with performance issues.

- *Funds-flow cycle (FFC).* A firm's funds-flow cycle is a determination of its cash flow, profitability and the investment required to achieve a given rate of growth. By assessing the requirements for capital (owners), the opportunity for leverage and the need to support a given sales volume with working capital and fixed capital, a firm's maximum growth potential can be determined. Tracking a company's FFC will allow the account team to assess any bottlenecks or financing gaps and should alert it to necessary measures that the client firm might need to take. Most importantly, this analysis will help determine in what way the global account team can contribute to the target business's growth and profitability.

- *Valuation.* Over the past few years a sense of a firm's market capitalization has become very important in assessing financial realities. Valuations are methods that attach a capital value to a business or firm, which might be in line with or at variance to the actual market capitalization. Financial analysts routinely publish such valuations, although some have recently been discredited as biased. Nevertheless, a sense of the valuation, compared to other firms against which the client company will be competing, will be part of the financial footprint assessment, as it will contribute to the understanding of where the company might move strategically.

We are not suggesting turning the global account team into chief financial officers. However, developments in business practice over the years have shown that financial savvy is part of the managerial set of competencies that are highly prized. In order to show how it can add value to a particular target client, the account team will be challenged to demonstrate this by referring to a set of financial indicators relevant to the client.

ASSESSING BUSINESS UNIT STRATEGY

Having mapped out the corporate environment, we now focus on the unit that will actually be the client, or target client, for our account team. We previously made the point that most account teams will not really face an entire corporation; rather, the client will be a sub-set or sub-unit of the corporation.

The business unit most closely associated with our account team is the one in need of further strategic assessment. In particular, we need to understand the content of the unit's strategy, its direction and goals. We will refer to the targeted business unit as 'the company' in all further parts of the analysis.

Undertaking a competitive assessment

Assessing the company's competitiveness may start with a perspective on its standing compared to that of directly competing firms. A common way to assess this is determining industry rankings or market share in either unit volume or sales. When such rankings are established, we need to be cognizant of the fact that a company may not compete in all sectors of a given industry. Competitiveness should also be assessed on a forward basis, with an eye on share development, and a view taken of top-line growth vs its competitors, not merely past performance. The account team not only needs to know where its client stands now, but also have an idea of future competitiveness.

One of the challenges of competitive assessment is the need to convey a picture on a global basis. Account teams are frequently knowledgeable about a firm's home-market strength because they are typically based on home-market sales teams with local knowledge. The purpose of the assessment for global account management is global, so share and volume data as well as projections should be established on a global basis.

Mapping segment coverage

Given the earlier analysis of industry segments, it will be necessary to understand how the target company covers or services its various segments. Segment coverage is an important measure of competitiveness and can easily be compared to other firms.

The account team will have had to work out an industry segmentation when reviewing its target client's industry. That work will pay off as it tries to establish segment coverage. The team will be able to tell if the client company has broad or narrow segment coverage, whether it acts as a specialist or a generalist and how this compares against its competitive peers. Documenting segment coverage will help assess how the company competes and will also indicate possible gaps that might trigger future actions. The information can be compared against the assessment of required market coverage and 'must segments' stemming from the industry analysis described earlier.

If a company is targeting several players from the same industry for its global account management approach, it is strongly suggested that a standardized segmentation scheme be used depicting all players in the industry. Such a methodology might come out of the earlier industry discussions and leverage the time and effort of multiple teams on different global firms in the same industry.

Charting product and service scope

Companies operate with varying product and service scope, which covers the breadth of their offerings. Product line breadth is related to but different from segment coverage. Through this information the account team can tell how a target client operates and competes. Again, a target client might be narrow or broad, focused or general. Understanding product breadth will help the account team assess client needs. Comparing the target client's product breadth with its competition and understanding the segments that must be covered will help the account team uncover possible opportunities to contribute to the company's strategy.

Knowing the value chain activity range

Not all players are likely to deploy themselves equally across the value chain, therefore the company's particular way of engaging in such activities is important. Depth of forward or backward integration, use of outsourcing or a particular philosophy can all contribute towards a deeper understanding. The earlier analysis of the industry on a macro and micro system basis will have yielded an understanding of how a target company should extend itself.

The first part of the analysis should cover the macro value chain or industry business system. Different firms exhibit different trends in terms of backward and forward integration. An account team needs to understand its target client's preference and strategy with respect to integration and how it influences a company's performance.

A separate set of data covers the micro value chain or the company's internal business system. Again, the same issues arise in terms of preferred integration. The account team should know its client's strategy with respect to core activities, outsourcing and emphasis in terms of resource allocation compared to its peers.

Understanding resource deployment along the micro business system

The account team needs to know where and how the target company invests its resources. Investment or expenditure against key value steps such as R&D, manufacturing, systems developments and market development is extremely important. Benchmarking against industry standards will yield additional insights that may serve as clues to the target company's next move. Even in industries that are viewed as mature it can be surprising how resource-allocation patterns differ among major players.

Firms may change their resource deployment over time and an account team needs to be aware of any impending changes. Some of these changes may reflect the preferences of a new management team, others may be a response to new challenges in an industry. Changing industry economics is also a major driver of such strategic shifts and can be used effectively by account teams to enhance their own positions.

Tracking geographic deployment

The account team should track geographic deployment across the global industry opportunity. Geographic deployment can be in respect of market coverage or the company's own resource deployment, such as factories. Both are important and can influence the shape of the global account management team's tasks.

Tracking geographic coverage will determine the markets in which the firm competes. The company's major markets need to be understood and the complete range of market deployment, such as salesforces, distribution centres or service centres is critical. This information can be cross-checked against the results of the earlier analysis on 'must segment' markets yielding important clues on impending moves. For any of the firm's key markets, it will also be a requirement to know the extent of its market position and competitive ranking by market. If a company has different product offerings in different markets, this is the time to address that aspect and integrate it into the overall analysis.

Aside from the target firm's market coverage, there will be a particular interest in determining its asset deployment for manufacturing, R&D and any other functions that may be of interest to the account team. If the account team is aiming to market raw materials, factory locations may be most important, as well as the location of the purchasing function. If the company is marketing IT products, the location of the client's IT function and facilities may be of special interest.

The dynamic aspects of the target company's behaviour are also of importance because they may signal areas for future moves. Can the team already see where new investments would be made and in which countries? Some firms tend to signal shifts in their geographic balance ahead of the game and publish their intentions in annual reports. Staying on top of potential strategic changes is part of the global account management team's responsibility.

Reviewing compliance against industry codes

In previous chapters we covered in depth the concept of an industry code and the need for a firm in any industry to meet its requirements. We have also encouraged account teams to analyse their company's industry in considerable detail. When analysing the business of any given global key account, it is time to take a detailed look at how the key account performs against the requirements of the industry code.

The purpose of this analysis is twofold. First, the account team needs to become conversant with the strategy of its account, as if it were an insider at the strategy-making level. This familiarity will make it easier to lead the direction of the account's strategy, rather than lag behind in reactions. Mapping out any gaps between requirements and current strategic behaviour is often a good indicator to help anticipate a company's moves. Secondly, the key account team will need to establish its credibility with the account. Demonstrating in its interactions that it is fully conversant with the account's industry requirements is a precondition for establishing a dialogue at the strategic level, as opposed to being relegated to interface at operational levels only.

Reviewing compliance with global logics

Analogous to the understanding of industry requirements is the need to review how well the target company conforms to the forces of global logic. The analysis described in the previous chapter calls for an unbiased view of the global logic forces and suggests that they apply to all industry players, the target account as well as its peers. Reviewing and comparing the company's actual behaviour in terms of global logic forces against the unbiased facts of the industry can lead to interesting conclusions that the account team can use when interacting with the client.

Since global account teams are invariably dealing with companies that have global operations, those clients tend to engage in an intensive debate about the appropriate level of globalization. The account team, equipped with its analysis, can discuss areas of potential over- or under-globalization. It can also view trends among the global logic forces and might be able to spot changes that eventually will force the client to change its strategy, its approach or its business mix.

A potentially rewarding approach consists of mapping the implied behaviour of the client firm and comparing its outward actions against the requirements of global logic forces. Some companies' behaviour can differ from the real requirements and any gaps are good indicators of future changes as companies bring their strategies more in line with needs. In other words, there is such a thing as 'perceived' global logic vs 'actual' global logic forces.

Sensing performance against dominant industry metrics

Earlier we described the value of understanding the dominant industry metrics in a given industry and the need to use them as benchmarks. In cases where the industry metrics are well known, the account team may want to concentrate on monitoring those values to keep score and to understand the target company's relative industry position. In industries such as retailing the dominant industry metrics, such as sales per square metre or cubic metre are usually well known and regularly reported in industry reports.

In other industries the actual definition of an industry metric may be much less clear, and it is conceivable that a global account team, through its experience with other related accounts, may have a particular insight into important or relevant metrics. In such a case, mere knowledge of the metrics becomes powerful information and the account team needs to make it known that it possesses insights that may be more penetrating than those of its client. At the very least, the account team should know about the performance metrics with which its client is concerned, again to demonstrate closeness to its business.

Projecting a growth path

There are a number of important issues to be examined when analysing an account's growth plan. Where is the company headed with its present strategy? Are there any clear signs of directions, implied or openly articulated? How does this influence future resource allocation for investments, assets, acquisitions, divestments and so on?

Since an account team needs to serve not only the present but also the future needs of its clients, obtaining a sense of the company's future direction is of great importance. Every company operates with a given strategy and the underlying forces of this strategy, assuming that it remains unchanged, will typically point in a certain direction.

An account team should get to the point where it is able to project the direction of growth beyond repeating only the facts that the company has released to the press. In terms of current strategy and resource allocation, where the company is going must be a question that an account team should be able to answer. From such an understanding, it may be able to project future sales or business volume.

Anticipating impending moves

Most companies have a strategy that allows the analyst to second-guess their next moves. What will those next moves be in terms of geography, product lines, technology, manufacturing, levels of integration and so on?

Projecting and anticipating future moves is the culmination of the process of getting to know the strategy. If the account team aims to become a strategic insider – and we clearly make the case that this is a requirement for success as a global account team – the team needs to get to the point where it can anticipate major moves before they occur or become common knowledge. An account team that is always surprised by its client's moves has not yet risen to the required level.

To help in its assessment, the account team may want to start from the present strategy and resource deployment, factor in those moves already announced, and review additional next moves that might be logical, in line with strategy or imposed by outside industry conditions. Segment moves, product line changes, country or geographic coverage and changes in value-chain integration are areas of which the team needs to be apprised. Additional important moves could be acquisitions or divestments. To serve a client globally in multiple locations will require the account team to anticipate moves so that its own resources will be deployed in line with future client needs, not just current ones.

Picturing the vector of choices

What are the growth opportunities if they are pictured in a single chart? List all potential directions that the firm might pursue, including new or different segments, customer groups, geographies, technologies etc. How far along is the firm with this resource deployment?

The CEO of a high-technology company once described the range of options that his firm faces as his 'crisis of opportunity'. The same metaphor applies to the situation of most companies. There are so many avenues in which growth can be pursued, but resources are limited. As a result, choices have to be made that invariably involve trade-offs. Clearly, a key account team serving a major client will need to be aware of those choices and demonstrate that it is conversant with the client's key options at a strategic or CEO level.

Although any firm will invariably face some unique opportunities or choices, there are nevertheless some common patterns that repeatedly emerge. For illustrative purposes, we will display below such a set of choices in 'star' form, with some vectors falling into the categories of product/segment choices, geographic choices, value-chain intensity and integration and functional emphasis, as illustrated in Figure 5.1.

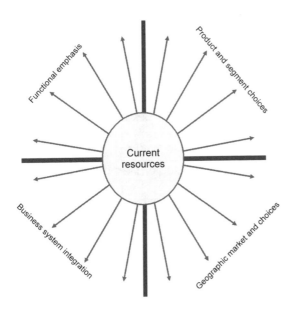

Figure 5.1 Charting options

- *Product or segment choices* cover the range of segments that the company currently covers and those that it might want to add.
- *Geographic choices* deal with the global reach of the company and its coverage or penetration of key markets, such as regional (Europe, North America, Asia, Latin America etc.) or by specific country if that makes more sense.
- *Value-chain intensity* concerns the macro business system and the company's chosen level of integration, either backward or forward. Choices might be to disengage or intensify in certain areas.
- *Functional emphasis* deals with the relative allocation of resources in such areas as R & D, manufacturing, marketing, sales, IT and so on and the choice of shifting resources from one area to another.

If we let a global account team display a company's choices in a chart as described above, we end up with the current resource deployment. For growth or improvement of its strategic position, any move to emphasize one vector or ray over another will tend to cause other areas to be omitted or deleted, in relative terms leading to fewer resources. Trade-offs between the various choices can be analysed and the account team will 'play CEO' as it reviews the options and rationalizes the choices. The company's own strategic moves will need to be consistent with the requirements of the industry codes and the global logic forces. Anticipated moves on the part of the client company can then be factored into the key account team's service strategy. This will lead directly to the client's strategic dilemmas.

Understanding the client's strategic dilemmas

Strategic dilemmas are similar to forks in the road: a decision has to be made as to which fork to take, but it is not always clear which one. In any industry companies face such dilemmas where a decision appears to be required in the form of a choice, but it is not always apparent how to resolve the dilemma.

Applied to a single global account, the account team needs to be aware of the major strategic dilemmas posed to the industry as a result of its exhaustive analysis of the industry business system. Each account or competitor, however, has its own strategic dilemmas that might turn out to be make-or-break decisions. This could involve a given level of integration in its business system or a required product or segment depth. Additional strategic dilemmas might be associated with a given company's strategy implementation.

Why should an account team get involved with its client's strategy to such an extent? This is clearly a relevant question in this context. What needs to be pointed out is that from our experience, working with many firms where we have helped develop either the system of account management or the capabilities of individual account managers, client firms place a premium on teams that understand their problems and strategic issues. Demonstrating knowledge of a client firm's strategic dilemmas is a proxy for 'customer orientation' or 'closeness to a client's business'. Such perceived closeness builds credibility and opens the door to more business. Beyond credibility, it also opens the supplying company's own mind to capturing new opportunities.

ASSESSING THE CURRENT BUSINESS

In the previous sections of this chapter our focus has been on understanding the target company's strategy. We have spent a considerable amount of effort on understanding that strategy, and some readers might suggest that we focused little if anything on selling any product or services to the account. At this juncture, we would like to turn our focus squarely to selling to the target account. Reviewing the account team's own business with the client, we will suggest approaches beyond the typical scorekeeping employed by most companies.

Establishing a sales penetration chart

Looking at the firm's activities, product lines, geographies and so on, how far has your firm penetrated the company compared to current and potential competition? This analysis should result as closely as possible in 'market share' by relevant product lines, as the data available permits.

We suggest that the team start with a set of sales statistics usually available to most account teams. The reason for this is to determine to what extent it has been able to penetrate the target customer and compare this against competition. In other words, the account team needs to know its market share for the entire account.

While this may sound simple, we have observed many firms who have great difficulties establishing this on a worldwide basis with any level of confidence. Account teams often work with sales and share figures from the head office team, the group focusing on the client's head office or main operation. When considering business in far-flung operations or other countries, the data is often limited or only partially available. Clients operating under different names in many countries make this process more difficult.

Market share estimates are also subject to fluctuations. While some client firms might assist by indicating global volumes and purchases from competitors, for many account teams such help will not be available. As a result, the account team will need to establish the data through painstaking searching and sharing of data on sales and other activities. In any event, a clear set of data covering both unit and revenue volumes by product or service lines will be the starting point.

Eventually, a thorough opportunity analysis for target clients in a given industry might lead to the creation of a 'customer loading factor', which can be defined as the ability to absorb or require the account team's products or services. This could be expressed in numeric terms and might be made comparable across other industries. It might also serve as the basis of analysis if a new client is to be a target for which no data is presently available.

Establishing the global sales opportunity

In order to guide strategy, account teams need to reflect on the potential or global opportunity that the account represents. Many account teams do not supply all of their firm's possible products or services to their target account. This may be for historical or political reasons, but if the situation persists over time the account team may start to lose sight of the total opportunity that would be theoretically available to it. The opportunity needs to be projected into the future given the account's intended or anticipated strategy, providing an adequate assessment of the longer-term business opportunity. Again, this opportunity should be seen from a global perspective, covering all of the client's global operations and potential business whether covered at this point in time or not.

A major benefit of having an accurate account of the present business and the entire global opportunity is the motivating factor on the team once the gap between opportunity and real business is demonstrated. In addition, account teams can be compared on their 'penetration ratios', the percentage of total opportunity captured, even if the accounts are of different sizes or structures.

Mapping the company's decision-making unit

One of the account team's most important responsibilities is to map the target client's decision-making unit governing its purchasing process. Since most account teams tend to be composed of seasoned sales executives with good purchasing and operations contacts, the risk of not fully appreciating the entire web of decisions is great. The decision-making unit is not only the direct interface with the account team, but includes a range of influencers, gatekeepers, specifiers and approvers who come together in an intricate way. Clearly, much of this is company or account specific and not industry specific. In many instances, the account team needs to come to an understanding of whether a given engineering product-adoption process is driven by its client's engineering department, the production department or the design department. For other products or services, similar assessments need to be made so that the team can more effectively share the information.

An additional aspect of the purchase decision-making process in a globally active company is the role of various administrative levels. Most large, global firms have a corporate purchasing function, as well as purchasing on divisional, SBU and/or regional as well as country levels. The roles and responsibilities of these units are frequently not readily visible to outsiders, although anecdotal knowledge exists among most key account teams. To achieve superior performance, the purchase decision process needs to be mapped out in detail so that it can be shared across the entire account team, many of them physically located in different parts of the world.

Understanding the client's purchasing philosophy

To some extent the purchasing philosophies of target clients are subject to the vagaries of fashion and managerial changes. When it comes to global operations, companies have a tendency to swing between centralization and decentralization, and this is often related to senior management changes.

In addition, however, it is clear from the practices of global firms that purchasing has risen in importance and companies do place a premium on relying on fewer suppliers. This is driven by an understanding that fewer but key suppliers can enter into a partnership for mutual benefit, and that client firms no longer rely solely on a supply relationship.

For a global key account team it is therefore important to understand the philosophy of the company in relation to supply arrangements. While it may not govern all of the customer's present actions, strong philosophies can become fixed in actual purchasing practices and policies over time. A key account team should be expected to know what the target client's view of global purchasing relationships is and how globally it intends to run its operations. This knowledge will also be valuable as the supplying company tries to assess for whom it should provide the global key account service, and if it should be a single service or one that is flexible and adjusts to the company's global purchasing practices.

Determining leverage points

Having understood the client's industry, strategy and internal organization concerning purchasing, the key account team will be able to arrive at some indications on how it can contribute to the success of its assigned account. Based on strategic understanding of the key account's business, the team needs to find what we call 'hooks' or leverage points that will allow it to make the client more successful in its industry. We understand that this is a tall order and we offer an example for illustrative purposes.

A European supplier of polyurethane chemicals tried to sell its more sophisticated formulation to car seat manufacturers. Its new product formulation was more expensive per seat and required a change in the seat manufacturers' production line. The seat manufacturers declined to make the switch. In discussions with the OEM, it became clear that car companies needed to differentiate their cars through interior design. Space for passengers was always at a premium. The new chemical formulation allowed for a thinner, less space-consuming seat, providing the car designers with a small advantage in additional headroom. When understood in the context of automotive OEMs and car design, this turned into a strategic advantage. Suddenly the extra room gained was more valuable than the additional cost per chemical expended in forming car seat cushions. The entire discussion turned from discussion of price per kilo for chemicals into helping the customer gain headroom in the car.

The supplier's contribution was viewed as strategic and it was able to supply a substantial amount of newly formulated materials. Clearly, if the chemical company had not understood the strategic value of additional space it might not have been able to convince its key account to switch. It brought its own expertise to bear on a key strategic issue for the customer. On the other hand the customer, as a seat assembler, did not have sufficient chemical expertise to know that this kind of breakthrough could be achieved, and in turn had not approached the chemical company with such a request.

Successful global account strategy thus depends increasingly on linking selling the firm's products or services to the strategic elements faced by the target client. The global account team must find areas where it can make a major contribution to the client's success. These areas are based on solid industry understanding and the client's strategic needs. There may be a few or several such hooks, which may add to the client's volume, efficiency or overall competitiveness and can be demonstrated as clear and compelling contributions.

Strategic selling vs product selling

From the above example and the book so far, the reader will understand that our proposed global key account management process is founded solidly on strategic understanding. As we have emphasized previously, this is based on the assumption that account teams with a deep strategic understanding of their customers' businesses or industries have a strong competitive advantage in shaping value propositions that can make a difference to the customer.

It must also be said that our approach favours strategic understanding over mere relationship management, sometimes referred to as 'wine and dine'. Our global key account management process obviously does not suggest that basic sales skills and relationship management, based in solid business behaviour, are not valid. We would merely like to point out that long-term competitive advantage cannot be built on relationships alone. We are increasingly in business environments where continual management changes have eroded the value and longevity of such relationships.

The risk of over-reliance on relationships was demonstrated by a large, global IT hardware supplier with extensive key account relationships to many large, global firms. In an effort at professionalization, the company had brought together many of its most important account managers on a programme during the spring of 2001. Many of these account managers managed substantial volumes sold to well-known companies in the banking, insurance, telecommunications and manufacturing sectors. Many had strong personal relationships with the top executives at their accounts and could justifiably be called well connected.

As the stock market changed and burst the dot-com bubble, however, it was amazing to see how quickly many of the accounts represented underwent substantial changes. Eventually this meant that the senior executives on whom the account managers were relying for contacts were forced out. For example, less than two months after the conclusion of the group meeting, companies such as Chase, JP Morgan, WorldCom, ATT, Lucent, Ericsson, DaimlerChrysler, Ford, ABB and others had experienced significant changes that had eliminated or devalued the pre-existing relationship. Turmoil in many industries, constant executive changes, mergers or acquisitions always challenge the account team, making an over-reliance on personal relationships alone difficult to sustain a long-term relationship.

THE PROCESS OF GLOBAL KEY ACCOUNT ANALYSIS

The reader will properly have concluded that the exercise we have outlined will require changes in most account teams' approach to their business. Each account team will also need to organize itself in such a way that strategic assessment tasks can be carried out without paralysing the important day-to-day business.

Clearly, the responsibility for such a process rests with the team's leaders. However, does a single team member have all the relevant facts immediately available? Instead, knowledge of a client firm and its industry or business is shared among many different individuals, each of whom might be contributing only a small piece to the overall puzzle. Leading the team to the knowledge that the individual puzzle pieces add up to the entire strategic position of the target client is an important task. It will take time and face-to-face meetings. Firms that tend to succeed in this have regular meetings where time is spent on strategic issues.

Accessing data sources

Good data sources will of course be of substantial help. The main sources are industry-level data and analysts' reports that have good industry coverage for all major players.

A second significant source is participant-specific data (bottom-up), which is contributed by the various account managers as they size up their own companies or accounts. This data would be assembled by the various account managers and presented in a fairly complete form at industry meeting(s).

The best data sources are annual reports, investment analysts' reports, industry articles and the results of ongoing meetings with the account. Do not forget the company's website for further information. Bring a good selection of information to the team meeting to analyze the global account's industry and strategy.

Gaining access to data that would answer many of the questions raised in this and the previous two chapters may appear daunting to many people. However, in today's freewheeling environment an amazing amount of data is openly available at no or low cost, ready for the person who makes an effort to obtain it.

In general there are three main sources of data: data covering the industry, data related to the account, and the account team itself. We have noted potential sources of data throughout the previous sections and will provide only a limited list below.

Data on the industry

- Investment analysts' reports, particularly those sections that cover the industry of an investigated company, not merely the company itself.
- Public information on industries by such sources as daily newspapers, weekly magazines etc., accessible through web-based search engines.
- Government-issued information or reports issued by semi-public agencies.
- General web-based information, although the user must be careful to make sure it is reliable.

Data on target client

- Investment analysts' reports, particularly those parts that focus on the target client. We suggest using several analysts, not just one, and watching out for inherent bias.
- Public information on companies by such sources as daily newspapers, weekly magazines etc., accessible through web-based search engines.
- Publications by the target company, including annual reports, SEC filings, websites and press releases.
- General web-based information, although the user must be careful when it comes to reliability.

Global account team as a source

- Assemble the knowledge of all account managers on the target company, including those in different international locations.
- Poll former account team members.
- Check with senior executives who may have had contact with the account.

Our general experience is that there is a wealth of information readily available, but that it will take time and effort to sift through non-essential facts to reach conclusions on which action can be taken.

THE BENEFITS OF FORMALIZING THIS PROCESS

The process outlined above requires an initial investment of time and is more formal than that practised by the typical account team. To institute such a process one has to be convinced that the benefits of its formality outweigh the time requirement. Once a company has adopted and institutionalized its global key account process, particularly on the analysis side, it can leverage the knowledge gained in several ways:

- *Leverage across the same industry.* Many companies have account teams that serve different players in the same industry, and some account teams may serve more than one key account. In those circumstances, the industry aspect of the analysis, particularly that described in Chapters 3 and 4, is identical and can be leveraged across several account teams. For example, if a company serves several pharmaceutical companies, only one set of pharmaceutical industry and global logic data is needed. A larger investment in quality data can be justified because it can be amortized over multiple accounts.

- *Leverage across multiple industries.* Although the content of course differs by industry, the approach is the same. Even though an account team may at times serve target clients in different industries, the familiarity gained during the industry overview will save time once additional industries are included. Alternatively, a company serving different industries might cluster its account teams by industry and have them share information as above.

- *Leverage across different companies.* Account teams often underestimate the power of leveraging industry experience across several players active in the same industry. Their clients that are active in one place only lack the perspective gained from serving several companies in a related industry. If that perspective can be harnessed, the experience of the account team, based on observations of multiple companies in the same industry, can be superior to the experience gained by the target client on the basis of one observation, its own company.

Institutionalizing the learning across the company

At this point the reader might gain the impression that we advocate a process of global key account management for individual teams only. While our descriptions and suggestions can be applied account by account, it should by now have become clear that substantial benefits would accrue to a company that is able to institutionalize this analytical

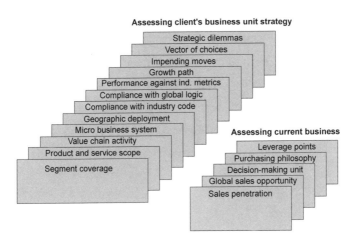

Figure 5.2 Battery of charts

approach. By doing so, the company would gain the benefits of not having to reinvent the wheel each time and obtain the leverage described above. More importantly, with executives being reassigned increasingly rapidly, the learning that comes to one team could be generalized if all teams applied a similar approach. Materials disseminated by one team could be more easily integrated and understood by others. Executives who find themselves in a leadership position and having to give guidance to many global key account teams would find it easier to absorb data or strategies across multiple accounts.

Consequently, just as a company has mandatory reporting and a standardized format for financial matters, it may also advocate standardized sets of materials that are to be used by all its account teams. For this reason we are including Figure 5.2, a sample 'battery' of charts that might be used as a basis for such a formalized process.

CONCLUSION

In this chapter we have outlined an extensive analytical approach that would make a global account team a strategic insider in its selected target account. Global key account management is more than that, however, and the following chapters will focus more on the managerial work that an account team needs to undertake, as well as the management processes that a company needs to put in place to make its account team effective.

Developing and Delivering the Value Proposition

6

As we have already seen, global account management (GAM) is an organizational approach to managing the interface between a global supplier and global customer. The process should significantly improve the effectiveness of the global sales effort in two ways. First, having a single point of contact to coordinate all interactions between suppliers streamlines communications and improves mutual understanding of each organization's objective and strategy. Second, the global account management structure allows the supplier the opportunity to focus its resources to create significant value for the global account through its global view of the account's industry, its strategy and its goals and objectives. This chapter will describe the process of developing and delivering value to global accounts.

SELECTING GLOBAL ACCOUNTS

Determining which customers the GAM programme will focus on is the first step in developing a value proposition. This discriminating process is counter to the 'more is better' school of customer acquisition. Global account management requires a comprehensive and coherent process for selecting global partners. This should include consistent criteria that establish a strategic/operational foundation for building effective global account relationships. In addition to providing a framework for the overall global account programme, the criteria should be flexible enough to accommodate companies with differing industry cycles and economic realities. Some criteria that have proven effective include potential partner's size, historical and projected growth rates, market potential, geographic locations, global purchasing, reputation, industry standing and willingness to partner. Underlying these criteria are, first, the need for the partner to be large enough to support the cost of a global account relationship, and second, the willingness to interact in a way where additional value can be created, beyond simple volume pricing.

Setting criteria for global accounts is an important step. These criteria are needed to develop a uniform understanding of what a global customer is. While all customers are important, many are not ready to operate globally. The criteria ensure that global customers are aligned with the company's corporate strategy and will receive the appropriate resources. Finally, global account selection criteria are needed to help ameliorate the turf wars that will arise as local sales managers see key customers being coordinated or handled by a global account manager.

There is a tendency to base the selection of global accounts on the current and potential size of the opportunity. While this is a necessary criterion, it must be accompanied by willingness on the part of the customer to partner with the supplier. This means that the global customer sees the supplier as a contributor to its success. This cooperation process is illustrated in Figure 6.1. The customer must be willing to discuss its strategy, its product-development plans and its view for the future. Global customers will only be willing to have this intimate relationship with a limited number of suppliers, which depends not only on the customer's view of the firm but also on how the customer views the product category. For example, a global chemical customer may consider it useful to have an intimate relationship with a logistics transportation company, while it may see less value in an intimate relationship with an electrical supplier.

Praxair is the largest industrial gas company in the Americas and third largest in the world. It has grown its number of global customers at 15 per cent a year. The company uses the following criteria to select global accounts (Kerestes, 1998):

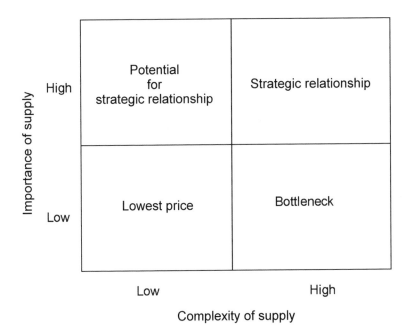

Figure 6.1 Purchaser's view of supplier's products or services

- Part of one of Praxair's strategic sectors.
- Investing in global growth.
- Number 1 or 2, market leader.
- Expected future revenue growth.
- Could leverage Praxair's global activities/knowledge.
- Praxair could obtain a preferred position.
- Account is global.
- Current share of account.
- Current revenue of account.

THE GLOBAL ACCOUNT TEAM

Once a global account has been selected, a global account team is usually formed that includes the people currently serving the global account and the global account manager. This team is discussed in the next chapter.

The global account manager and team start by reaching out to the potential global account and building on existing relationships. Usually the team builds on an existing relationship because the selection criteria frequently require the client company to have historical and projected revenue and growth with the supplying company. The relationship between the global account management team and the global account, particularly mutual trust, is a determining factor in building and developing the value proposition.

Engaging the customer when creating and managing a plan for an existing or new global account will align expectations and build trust. When developing a new global account, key members who will be handling and interacting with the account should come together to develop a coordinated plan. Each global account plan should detail the objectives, goals, strategies and measurements to be used. During the planning process and in periodic assessments, the customer's participation should be maintained to ensure that the strategy of the account team and the global account are aligned to create maximum value. This engagement with the client group will provide the foundation for developing the value proposition by building trust and make the delivering of the value proposition easier.

Developing a value proposition in a GAM programme requires participation from the supplying company's clients. This may sound obvious but, like most relational interactions, it requires a fair amount of time and energy to develop before delivery.

GLOBAL VALUE PROPOSITION

Delivering superior global value is the essence of a successful GAM programme. Superior global value is directed towards a specific global customer within a specific time period, as illustrated in Figure 6.2. The global value will be superior to competing alternatives and will create a specific and measurable favourable result for the customer. The in-depth understanding of the global customer's needs will reduce the time taken to deliver superior global value, which may often not be recognized by local suppliers.

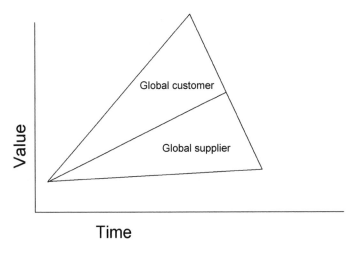

Figure 6.2 Delivering global value

Development of the value proposition requires an intimate understanding of the intended resulting experience for which the global account client is looking in the supplying company's products and/or services. This is challenging because it requires the supplying company to figure out the value proposition's time frame, the customer for the resulting experience, and the return for providing the experience and competing alternatives.

A benchmark study of 58 firms determined that accounts are willing to pay for four broad categories of value: technology, processes, administrative services that reduce costs, and sales and marketing support (NAMA, 1997).

Customers place a high value on technology that is core to their business results but not within their capabilities. For example, Occidental Chemical has developed a portfolio of high-technology, value-added services such as technical support, logistics, product management and R&D, which its customers value highly.

Customers also value processes that boost their productivity by improving quality, reducing overheads and producing measurable savings. For example, Marriott has developed a process to train travel agents on its bookings, product knowledge, service knowledge and consultative skills to serve its customers better. This process improves the individual travel agent's productivity as well as the entire agency's profitability.

In addition, customers value administrative services that reduce cost and improve profit. For example, Boise Cascade Office Products developed an information system that allows customers to review pricing, delivery, service and remedial action independently at any time.

Sales and marketing support that leads to increased sales is also valued by customers. For example, AC Delco has an advertising campaign supporting a strong brand that, combined with other retail support, boosts sales growth (NAMA, 1997).

The development of the value proposition is intricately connected with its delivery. As part of the development process, the supplying company needs to evaluate if it has the capabilities actually to deliver the value proposition. There are four vehicles for delivering the value proposition in a GAM programme: relationship, product/service, logistics and communications. Each of these vehicles will be discussed later in the chapter.

If the supplying company finds that it lacks competence in one of these four, the development of the value proposition should halt and a decision be made on whether to acquire the lacking capability, develop a new value proposition within existing competencies or terminate the entire project. Global account management is a business proposition that aims at improving the global client's real business experiences within its own operations and extending to its customers. Understanding the full scope of the global client's business experiences will set a GAM programme on the right track to developing the value proposition.

Criteria for a resulting experience

A resulting experience (Lanning, 1998) is:

- An event, or sequence of events, physical and/or emotional, which happens in the customer's life because of doing what some business proposes.

- The end-result consequence of this event for the customer.
- Either superior, equal or inferior in comparison to a customer's alternative experience.
- The value for the customer of this relative consequence.
- Specific and measurable: one can objectively determine if the customer experienced the events, consequences and value compared to alternatives.

Armstrong World Industries example

Understanding the resulting experience was critical in Armstrong World Industries' successful global relationship with Citibank (SAMA, 2001). In 1999 Armstrong, a global group that designs and manufactures floors, ceilings and cabinets, approached Citibank and started a preliminary partnership process. It conducted a high-level needs analysis to discover Citibank's critical issues in building materials and its suppliers. Armstrong discovered that Citibank met its three criteria: brand recognition and leadership in its industry, the potential to generate $500 000 annually to Armstrong, and the willingness and ability to collaborate and enter into a sole-sourcing supplier relationship.

Armstrong continued to conduct a thorough analysis. This analysis determined what sort of value Armstrong might offer Citibank; where Citibank was doing business around the world; and what the bank was looking for from suppliers in each of its regions. After developing a clear picture of Citibank's global needs, Armstrong presented it with a menu of customized services and capabilities that reflected Citibank's specific resulting experience needs. These included:

- Global single sourcing: dealing with one supplier globally.
- A match between Citibank's geographic needs and Armstrong's geographic presence, so that someone could own the local relationships as the global account manager owns the global relationship.

- On-time delivery. Logistics is one of Armstrong's core competencies. Products are delivered within 30 minutes of the time promised 97 per cent of the time.
- 15-year warranties on ceiling material.
- 10-year guaranteed availability of ceiling material.
- The ability to recycle some ceiling material. Citibank saw this as an excellent opportunity to cut costs and fulfil its own environmental policies.
- A complete quality-training curriculum, developed by Armstrong, available to any strategic account.
- The ability to institute e-commerce and electronic data interchange.
- A technical services group including an acoustician who could show how a combination of ceilings, furniture and sound masking can improve worker productivity.

Armstrong focused on Citibank's experience needs and issues specific to building materials and was able to develop a GAM plan that had a direct consequence for Citibank's resulting experience. Specifically, it addressed Citibank's experience needs in terms of logistics, recycling, training and technical services, in order to reduce supply chain costs and significantly improve worker productivity.

DEVELOPING A GLOBAL ACCOUNT MANAGEMENT CULTURE

The development of a constructive value proposition for global customers requires the successful implementation of a GAM programme in the supplying company. The subject of global account management implementation could be another book on its own. Many factors involved in implementing a single programme are unique to each company. To add to the complexity, each client within a single company's programme has its own specific issues.

Culture, for example, is a significant aspect of the implementation of a GAM programme that needs to be addressed. Each company has its own unique culture. Some decentralized global companies have significant cultural differences that vary depending on the national or geographic location of the business units. Couple the unique cultural situations within a global company with the national and geographic cultural variations around the world and quickly the cultural complexities that need to be addressed in implementing global account management become quite dynamic. Without a doubt, the issues around cultural complexity will never vanish; instead, they need to be continually managed.

Internally, companies first need to align cultures that will allow the successful implementation of a GAM programme. Citibank has transformed its culture to function on a global platform and has been able to focus on providing global account solutions that transcend traditional geographic and product boundaries, requiring a high degree of internal coordination and alignment between product and geographic divisions.

Marriott International (MI) example

In 1996 a CEO-sponsored taskforce created to analyse the effectiveness of the salesforce at Marriott International (MI) led to the development of a customer relationship management (CRM) programme (SAMA, 2002). The CRM programme in turn led to a sales transformation programme in 1997. This transformation programme consolidated the sales division, marketing division and customer services function into one reporting structure and business unit, except for the international salesforce. International sales continued to report to international operations.

The organizational transformation included the creation of a strategic accounts division within the sales and marketing division. This was responsible for MI's global and US-headquartered national accounts, which consisted of approximately 1500 commercial customers and annual sales of roughly $3 billion. The strategic accounts division overlays the hotels' salesforces and builds account teams around qualified commercial customers. In the course of the transformation, MI also consolidated Marriott.com, worldwide reservations, agency sales and field sales under the sales and marketing division.

Before MI had instituted the transformation process and new account management strategy, individual hotels acting alone to create demand handled their own sales and marketing. A system-wide salesforce of 225 000 sold on behalf of individual properties.

For the alliance programme to begin properly, MI had to sell the idea internally. It faced the challenge of moving the salesforce from a traditional transactional structure to an organization focused on account solutions. Since each hotel in the MI system was franchised and managed locally and each had a separate P&L statement, consolidation of account management was initially seen as a loss of control by individual hotel management.

To address this issue, MI conducted an internal campaign focused on selling the account strategy programme. Communication of the vision, mission and plan was continuous. For every presentation that was given to an external customer selling the account management strategy, three presentations were given to those involved internally. The GAM programme was mainly concerned with meeting the needs of strategic accounts and not with filling rooms at individual hotels.

During the account management formation and early stages of execution, MI continually communicated the urgency of change and every success was celebrated and communicated to all involved. This was achieved through e-mails relaying real success stories and praising work that encouraged and advanced strategic selling. MI brought in customers and conducted one-to-one presentations to help transform the sales team. Quarterly updates were conducted during business reviews. In the first year alone, the vice-president of alliance sales conducted over 80 internal meetings addressing alliance accounts. Sales training classes for more than 500 people were held every year specifically to demonstrate how strategic account management would change each job in the company.

By 1999, MI's salesforce had been completely overhauled and organized around customers, instead of around properties. At the time MI employed over 10 000 sales and reservation associates, all of whom carried out booking requests for any MI property worldwide.

Marriott's implementation of a GAM programme required significant internal cultural change. In order to serve its business customers more competitively, the company knew that it needed to make this change. Its successful implementation and, sequentially, operation of the programme required it to address and change its internal culture.

Success in a global account management programme

Many factors need to be considered in the implementation of a GAM programme. Some of these are culture, compensation, organizational structure and the global competitive environment. Christoph Senn has formulated a conceptual framework for implementing global account management by combining static and dynamic perspectives (Senn, 1999).

Three working levels are important from the GAM implementation static perspective:

- *Strategic level*: long-term business relationships with selected partners. This level occurs when companies decide to enter long-term partnerships with selected global customers. Time is critical because it is needed to develop the relationship and coordinate the two organizations working together globally.
- *Operational level*: consistent global business solutions. This level combines the product and service offerings into one package to benefit the global accounts.
- *Tactical level*: the evolving adaptation of management structures to the customer network. This level deals with putting the right people in the right place at the right time.

Three working levels are important from the GAM implementation dynamic perspective:

- *Step 1*: Define goals and objectives together with global accounts. Both the supplier company and the customer company objectives need to be aligned, which often is best achieved through a joint GAM meeting of both supplier and customer employees.
- *Step 2*: This step consists of suppliers adjusting their business process to reflect the structure of their global accounts through a thorough analysis of the value chain/network. This may result in business focus changes and lead to new business opportunities.
- *Step 3*: The third step entails companies institutionalizing a learning process that captures the knowledge of their business with global accounts. This requires an information system that allows global account information to be distributed ubiquitously.

In combining the static and dynamic perspectives, Senn provides a conceptual framework that has a process-oriented perspective (Table 6.1). This conceptual construction illustrates nine key decisions points for implementing a GAM programme (Senn, 1999).

UNDERSTANDING THE GLOBAL CUSTOMER'S NEEDS

In developing the global account value proposition, it is helpful to have a complete understanding of the level of problems that the customer is facing globally. Kevin Wilson developed the PPF Model (Product, Process and Facilitation), which is outlined below and can be used to explain the impact of problem resolution in the global account relationship (Wilson, 1999a):

Table 6.1 A conceptual overview of global account management implementation

	Step 1	Step 2	Step 3
Strategic level	Business partners	Relationship management	Learning processes
Operational level	Products and services	Task management	Measurement of success
Tactical level	People	Management structures	Information management

- *Product-related problems.* Level one addresses the issues of customers finding solutions to problems through utilization of a specific product. These product-related problems are solved by utilizing the product's performance and conformance to specifications.
- *Process-related problems.* Level two addresses a commercial relationship that is integrated whereby the product or service provided by the supplier is incorporated into the buyer's value-creation process. The product, its delivery and the services associated with it all have a direct impact on the customer's use of the product and services. Problems associated with this integration are process-related problems.
- *Facilitation-related problems.* Level three deals with buyer/seller relationships, which can be classified as facilitation-related problems. These are related to the alignment of the supplier's and customer's strategic objectives, the creation of value for both parties, and the development of trust with the integration of systems and personnel.

The development of the value proposition requires long-term global relationships to be built within the supplying company and between the supplying company and the global customer. The first relationship building that needs to take place is within the supplying company's global operations. When the GAM programme is installed, the GAM team must immediately begin to build and/or expand trusting relationships with locally based company employees around the world. The success of the programme depends on how it is executed and operated around the world. Therefore, the global/local relationships within the company must be healthy. This may involve a significant cultural change, because the instigation of a GAM programme may be perceived locally as a loss of power and control of the business.

In order to start building the global/local relationship, it is important to include key local or regional employees in the GAM planning meeting and to keep them well informed of the progress of the programme. When the time comes to rely on local business divisions to carry out an aspect of the programme or assist locally with a GAM customer, they will be fully educated and informed about the GAM programme. It is also important that the members of the GAM team have developed a relationship with their company's varying local resources and knowledge bases and strengthen their level of access to them before trying to deliver a value proposition to a global account. The supplying company should also develop an understanding of the client company's local resources and its level of ability to receive a GAM value proposition locally.

The development of the internal local/global relationship is an aspect of GAM that is a struggle for many companies. Formal mechanisms can be designed to ensure that the global/local relationship is fostered and conflicts avoided.

An executive vice-president of global accounts for a global IT company commented as follows concerning the formal mechanisms in the internal global/local relationship (Hennessey, 2002):

> We continue to have it. I think every company has it. You cannot escape that. But with this international organization I am part of as well as the sector management process that we have set up we have got escalation points that people can give to people that can help them to get those local issues out of the way. Because sometimes it does come up and in our business the way it normally comes up would be not able to get resources focused on a particular project at a particular point in time. For example, let us say that you are working with a large global financial institution as your customer and they are implementing a set of software and hardware programs globally. Therefore, people have to go in and install the hardware work with the customer to get the software up and running etc. etc. The people that do that are going to be the local people. When a global account team is trying to align the company's resources with the global customer needs, even small installations must be considered. So when conflict of resources comes up we just make sure we have the right escalation processes in place to get it resolved so that we can do the right thing for the global customer.

The execution of the GAM programme and the success of specific global accounts will often depend on the global relationships with local employees that the GAM team members build within their company,

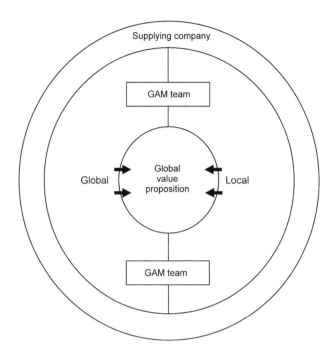

Figure 6.3 Delivering the global value proposition

visualized in Figure 6.3. This is important because frequently the GAM team members have no direct authority over local employees and business. This means that they have to manage through relationships and influence and not through direct reporting authority.

The internal global/local relationship is extremely important in developing a successful GAM value proposition. Equally important is developing a strong relationship with the global account. Some companies take a proactive stance with GAM programmes and work with their global customers, while others may be forced into it by customer demand, which is the most common. Whatever way the GAM programme comes into being, it is important that both supplier and global account customers have a strong working relationship entrenched globally throughout both organizations. This is a long and very expensive process, but it is critical to the success of the programme.

In most cases the global supplier/customer relationship needs to be familiar to both parties well before the introduction of a GAM programme. Most GAM relationships are not new to either the supplying or client company. There has usually been an existing working relationship on a local, national and regional level, and occasionally on an international level, for a significant amount of time. What is new is that these companies have not worked together on a global basis. The criteria for selecting a GAM account from the supplier's point of view include size, historical and projected growth rates, market potential, geographic locations, global purchasing, reputation, industry standing and willingness to partner. These all require that the potential global account and the supplier company already have a working relationship. This existing working relationship is what needs leverage in order to develop a value proposition successfully through the framework of a GAM relationship.

DEVELOPING THE RELATIONSHIP

The development of the GAM relationship and value proposition is usually the domain of the supplying company but is instigated by the client company. This requires a fair amount of outreach on the part of the supplying company. The most successful way to start to transform the supplier/customer relationship into a true GAM relationship is to bring the customer into the strategic account planning process. Since the GAM relationship usually finds its origins in a sales culture, this may require a significant shift in how the relationship is conceptualized and acted on. This move requires the supplier/customer GAM relationship to be integrated and thought of as strategic and not as a sales medium. Bringing the customer into the account planning process benefits both the customer and supplier in terms of building the GAM relationship by facilitating trust building between key individual team members on both sides of the relationship.

Examples of engaging the customer in the account planning process

At Fritz, a specialist in global integrated logistics, account teams hold quarterly meetings in which key account team members meet with representatives from the account and together analyse the last quarter's performance, evaluating problems, determining what is and what is not working and making necessary changes. After the meetings they hand out a written list of action items for all involved to follow. These will be reviewed and changed, as appropriate, at the subsequent quarterly meeting.

A large global bank and financial services company conducts annual relationship reviews with its global account clients and also involves them in the relationship planning process, which assists in setting mutual objectives for the client and the company when first developing the global relationship. The company also engages the customer in the account planning process through an intranet system developed to support the global customer marketing process that links the entire global account team for each global customer around the world. This helps the individuals on the supplier and customer sides to get to know each other better, understand each other's business challenges and provide an environment where value can be created. It also provides a forum for the supplying company to evaluate the seriousness of the customer's intent in regard to building a GAM relationship. This is an important issue, because a great deal of time and money can be wasted if one party in building the GAM relationship is not thoroughly committed and it is best to find this out early on.

A key aspect to this level of GAM relationship building is the knowledge opportunities that are opened up as the relationship develops. Sometimes the supplying company can help improve business situations for the global account customer that the latter did not even know were an issue. The development of the GAM relationship needs to happen at many different levels for both the supplier and customer companies. This is the means by which both companies involved in the relationship will take the process seriously and ensure that the relationship creates value. The relationship is best played out and developed through many different stakeholders.

It may be obvious to point out that the global account manager needs continually to build and lead the relationship with the client

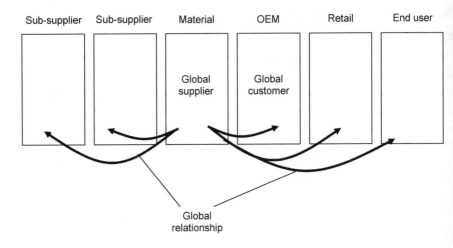

Figure 6.4 Potential global relationships of a global supplier

company. However, what may not be so obvious are the different relationships that may have to be developed. The global account manager will usually cultivate a strong relationship with a contact individual at the client company, who will frequently be at the purchasing or operational management level. It is equally important for the global account manager to build a relationship with individuals and teams who use the supplying company's products or services. This relationship should be one that facilitates productive comments and suggested improvements from the customer. In addition, it may be necessary for the global account manager to develop a relationship with the end user of the supplied product or service, as demonstrated in Figure 6.4.

In business-to-business relationships the product or service that the global account manager supplies may be incorporated into another product or service by the global account and several steps away from the end user. Developing a relationship with the end user will provide the global account manager with a valuable view of the whole supply chain in which the company competes. It also increases the probability that the supplying company will be better able to serve its global account customer, because it will have a full understanding of the industry and the relevant issues that the end user is attempting to address.

The global account manager also should develop relevant relationships across the customer's company in order to understand its cultural, political and business climate. This will help the global account manager better understand the client company's operations, business process and decision process. This understanding will help GAM relationships because the global account manager will be able to comprehend, foresee and adapt to changes in the customer's company. The size, in terms of volume and revenue, and global reach of a GAM relationship mean that the global account manager should be acutely aware of political situations that will arise, inside his or her own company and the customer company, relating to the global account.

The global account manager is not the only one who should be developing relationships with the global account customer. Executive-level relationships should parallel and support this work. The formation of executive-level relationships is important on several fronts. First, it shows internally that the supplier company is serious about the GAM programme and that it not only has executive support, but also executive involvement. Second, it demonstrates that the global account customer is taken seriously and is important to the supplier company. Third, the executive-level relationship also creates a medium that can prevent and solve problems that may develop at other levels in the GAM relationship. The executive involvement in the GAM relationship keeps the executives in both the customer's and supplier's company active and abreast of critical global business activities and relationships that are continually evolving in both companies.

The global account director for a global shipping and logistics company commented as below on executive involvement in the GAM relationship (Hennessey, 2002):

Each one of the global accounts has an executive sponsor. So, someone from my level in the company on up is assigned to just be the executive sponsor, the person who can cut through red tape. It is a court of last resort beyond the first two levels of management with whom they normally deal. It could be the CEO of North America; it could be the CEO of Europe. It would be beyond two levels of management of what is normally experienced. That makes it clear to everybody else in the company that there is sponsorship. This executive sponsorship facilitates many issues being worked out at the lower levels since everyone understands our commitment to global accounts.

Developing the value proposition for GAM requires an understanding of the complex nature of business relationships, cultures (business, national and regional), managing without direct influence and understanding the global account's resulting experience expectations. There is variation among the value propositions that one company will offer to its specific global accounts. The same value proposition does not work for every global account and as the GAM relationship matures so will the value proposition.

RESPONDING TO CHANGING CUSTOMER NEEDS

Delivering the value proposition in a GAM program is a dynamic and continually changing endeavour. As the two companies involved in the GAM relationship change from focusing on the transaction to focusing on the strategic relationship, the original value proposition will undoubtedly reflect this change. Any change in the value proposition will also change its delivery. Since the GAM teams are the primary vehicle for delivering the value proposition, this requires teams to be structured in a way that enables them to be responsive throughout the client company's organization and have the capability to evolve reflecting changes in the client's business, market forces and the GAM relationship.

The following case illustrates how the GAM team is the primary instrument for delivering the value proposition.

Solectron example

Solectron is an $18 billion electronic manufacturing service (EMS) provider that designs, manufactures, delivers, repairs and supports products for its partners (LaNasa, 2002). The company has 70 sites and more than 55 000 employees worldwide, with clients such as IBM, Hewlett-Packard, Cisco, Sun, Nortel and Sony. In 2002 it held the number one position in the EMS industry.

Customer teams at Solectron were an outgrowth of the organization's high level of customer focus and the need to manage the increasing complexity of both the supply chain and Solectron's offerings across geographies. Solectron uses customer teams to deliver its customer-focused value proposition to the largest global technology companies.

The company attributes much of its success to its global account management programme and partnership mentality. The foundation for success in partnering and building its global account programme is a high level of focus, commitment and passion for the customer. All levels of the organization from CEO to factory-line workers live by the motto 'Customer First'.

Solectron has a long history of making the customer its top priority. The first CEO, Winston Chen, made customer focus part of the fabric of the organization. He stressed the importance of understanding customer needs and working relentlessly to satisfy and exceed their expectations. The current CEO maintains Chen's legacy of the 'Customer First' philosophy. He has a working CEO-to-CEO level relationship with all key customers.

When the current CEO joined the company in 1988, his vision was to provide high-tech customers with a total 'one-stop shopping' solution, from design, manufacturing and delivery to repair and customer support. To deliver on this value proposition, Solectron has made strategic acquisitions to broaden its capabilities across the value chain. Under the current CEO's leadership, it grew from $3.2 billion in 1996 to $18.7 billion in revenues for 2001.

Solectron's first global account was Cisco Systems in 1996. Cisco had little interest in manufacturing and relied on providers, like Solectron, as an essential part of its supply chain. The Cisco global customer team began with only two members at the global level: the global account executive and the global account manager. Solectron has continued to expand and develop the Cisco global customer team.

Global account teams are developed based on two key criteria: potential revenue and complexity. Today the company has 15 global customer teams comprising approximately 75 per cent of its revenue. The teams are truly cross-functional at the global level and most team members are dedicated to one account. Operations, sales, finance, marketing and new product introductions (NPI) are key functions typically represented on the teams and report to the global account manager, as shown in Figure 6.5. Finance focuses on understanding the total cost of operations. Marketing is charged with understanding the competition and market sectors. New products are essential to Solectron's high-tech customers who are battling short product life cycles. To meet and exceed customers' expectations, Solectron added a new position, a director of new product introductions (NPI). As soon as the customer identifies a new product, the NPI director is responsible for driving design and development. The teams are designed around an understanding of customer needs and priorities and built to reflect specific customer strategies. Each customer is different; one size does not fit all.

Senior management was involved and committed to the global customer team concept from the start. In 2002, a global account executive (GAE) and a global account manager (GAM) managed each global customer team. In the past GAEs were corporate officers or senior executives with other responsibilities within the company.

Figure 6.5 Cross-functional customer team

Source: Adapted from LaNasa, Julie (2002) 'Solectron: Building customer teams to deliver on your company's value proposition', *Velocity*, Quarter 1, pp. 323–6.

Table 6.2 Evolved customer team model

Global account executive	Global account manager
Develop customer strategy	Manage P&L
Identify growth opportunities	Identify and understand customer's imperatives, goals and objectives
Build senior-level relations	
Develop integrated planning	Develop and implement effective account plans and strategies
Partnerships	Manage interface between customer and operations
Cross-business unit coordination	
Facilitate decision making both internally and externally	Lead cross-functional teams
	Architect asset/resource distribution

Source: Adapted from LaNasa, Julie (2002) 'Solectron: Building customer teams to deliver on your company's value proposition', *Velocity*, Quarter 1, pp. 323–6.

Realizing the complexity of its global customer relationships, Solectron evolved the GAE to a full-time position. A full-time executive, typically a seasoned vice-president, is needed to help customers react to economic conditions as quickly as possible.

The role of the GAE is to steer the ship. GAEs are ultimately responsible for the growth and success of global customers, as shown in Table 6.2. In addition to managing the P&L, one of the GAE's most important responsibilities is to identify opportunities to drive profitable growth for the customer and Solectron. This is done by the GAE reading articles, analysts' reports, press releases and financial statements that help them understand the global account's strategy and zero in on potential opportunities for both companies. The GAE also interacts with people at all levels across both organizations to identify new opportunities and clarify and shape new ideas for growth. In addition to identifying growth opportunities, another important responsibility of the GAE is to resolve conflicts and expedite decision making. Solectron recently decided that it was in the best interest of the customer to move production for a mature product from California to Asia to reduce costs. In the past this could have taken weeks and even months to execute internally, but with the GAE's high-level relationships and operating experience within Solectron, the change was made in a matter of days.

The GAE plays a key role in developing and negotiating some of Solectron's most complex customer acquisitions and evolving the customer's strategy. The GAE's key role is to develop a working relationship with the CEO of each of his or her major customers.

As the teams have evolved and increased in number, Solectron has added a vice-president of global accounts to act as a coach and mentor to each global account manager. The vice-president of global accounts assists in identifying best practices and improving processes for global customer teams. The global account managers continue to have a direct reporting relationship to the GAE.

Cultivating talent is a continuing focus of Solectron. Global customer teams require well-rounded and seasoned managers to act as global account managers and global account executives. This takes time and planning to ensure that people have the right experience. The CEO has appointed a vice-president of leadership talent to ensure that Solectron is cultivating the talent it needs.

DELIVERING THE VALUE PROPOSITION

The successful delivery of a GAM value proposition is rooted in the supplier company's ability to communicate the value that GAM is creating for the client company and solicit feedback from the client company. This communication is important because it provides a forum in which both companies can improve the value proposition. This communication should occur throughout both companies. If the value proposition is well communicated to a regional bloc or in a company's headquarters but not throughout the relevant stakeholders globally, then its delivery will be inadequate.

The value proposition delivery system within a GAM programme obviously starts with the strategy of both the supplying company and the client company. The GAM value proposition should include a time frame (for both implementation and delivery), the intended customer (a specific group within the client company or the client's customers), customer alternatives and the intended resulting experience that the client company should receive from the programme. How this value proposition will be provided then needs to be conveyed.

For example, if a proposed GAM value proposition was to provide a single point of contact and consistent product quality globally, then the way this would be provided to the client company is via a dedicated global account manager who handles the client exclusively and offers products for this specific client using standard quality and operating procedures. The way the GAM value proposition is communicated is to have the global account manager executing the role as a single point of contact, meeting often with the client company and allowing the client to visit manufacturing plants around the world and have it see for itself the standard quality and operating procedures.

Delivering the value proposition in a GAM programme requires the understanding of the process of developing the value proposition to be put into action. This understanding is illustrated in Figure 6.6. A majority of the value proposition delivery is through the GAM team and its surrounding services. Most GAM

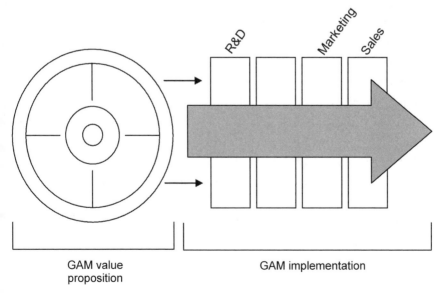

GAM value
proposition

GAM implementation

Figure 6.6 Implementing global account management

relationships are built from an existing business rapport, so one can imply that what is at stake in delivering the value proposition is not the supplier's product but the services, knowledge base and customization associated with that product. Delivering the value proposition in terms of GAM is about providing the global account, and its customers, with information that makes the product easier and less expensive to use, maintain, order, deliver, repair and manage globally. These operational and logistical needs can often be delivered through product customization.

Steelcase example

Steelcase International, a global office furniture manufacturer and service provider, delivers its GAM value proposition through its Global Alliances structure (Hennessey, 2002). Steelcase's Global Alliances is the group that executes its GAM strategy and delivers the GAM value proposition to its global accounts. The Global Alliances programme is charged with leveraging the global organization's knowledge, product and service position to meet the demands of its global accounts.

Steelcase's global customers face issues that many companies confront when they expand into global business. Some of these challenges include multiple locations across the world, different country standards and code requirements, different work cultures, a mobile workforce and a blending of different organizational structures. These issues resulted in Steelcase's global customers demanding that the company lead the global relationship, ensure that they have access to its knowledge, product and services, providing consistency across both organizations and delivering an integrated solution. The value proposition that Steelcase's Global Alliances delivered reflected the organization's understanding of the issues with which its global accounts were confronted when doing business around the world.

Delivering Steelcase's Global Alliances value proposition to customers involves the following:

- *Focused representation.* Steelcase provides a single point of contact to lead a team aligned to its Global Alliances customer's key business locations and within a global matrix.
- *Steelcase leads the strategic relationship* between its enterprise and its Global Alliances customers and translates their issues across their enterprise to bring to bear Steelcase's full capability in support of global workplace needs.
- *Executive sponsorship.* Steelcase ensures that the Global Alliances customers' issues are heard and dealt with at the highest levels within the company. An 'executive sponsor' participates in the strategic relationship between Steelcase and the global account.
- *Priority order fulfilment.* All orders will be managed through the Global Alliances order fulfilment process, assuring priority attention to global account orders.
- *E-commerce.* Automating the relationship is a high priority and Global Alliances customers are assured priority in establishing new e-commerce platforms.
- *Knowledge exchange.* Transforming the ways Global Alliances customers' people work is a function of applied knowledge. Global Alliances customers have direct access to Steelcase's experts and its knowledge resources.

Steelcase was able to deliver its value proposition because it understood its global customers' business problems in terms of services, knowledge base and customization associated with its products (McCann, 2001a).

VEHICLES FOR DELIVERING THE VALUE PROPOSITION

Delivering the value proposition within a GAM programme turns the abstract concepts behind the value proposition into tangible products, services and, most importantly, relationships that are mutually profitable in the long term.

There are four vehicles for delivering the value proposition in a GAM programme: relationship, product/service, logistics and

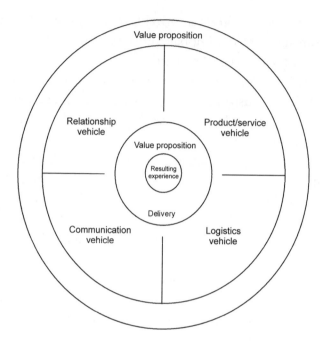

Figure 6.7 Delivering global value

communications. Because each vehicle is intricately connected with the others, the order in terms of sequence or importance depends on the specifics of the individual programme (Figure 6.7).

Delivering the product/service

The product/service vehicle for delivering the value proposition consists of providing a physical product and/or performing a service within the context of a GAM relationship that meets the client's intended resulting experience expectations. Providing a product or a service is the most obvious way to deliver the value proposition. This is simply when the client company goes through with the purchase of the supplying company's product and/or service and uses this as a vehicle to achieve an intended business result. Within a GAM programme the product/service vehicle is customized, through the GAM relationship, to meet the client company's unique intended results. This concept of product/service features is easy to recognize and is utilized to some extent in all business transactions. Since GAM is as much about strategic relationships as it is about products and services, the product/service feature for delivering the value proposition needs to recognize this, thus making it a product/service/ relationship vehicle.

Managing the relationship

The relationship vehicle aspect of delivering the value proposition is important to understand because GAM programmes are usually instigated in the context of existing business dealings. Before a programme is started, the potential GAM customer in most cases already has experienced varying aspects of the supplying company's products and/or services and value proposition with, at least, a material degree of satisfaction. With GAM, the relationship between the two participating companies is as important in delivering the value proposition as the product/service vehicle. Why is this?

GAM programmes are always built in the context of enhancing an existing product and/or service, so it would be easy to mistake it for another service within the product/service vehicle. The real enhancement in delivering the GAM value proposition is the long-term strategic relationship developed between the two companies involved, as illustrated in Figure 6.8. Not surprisingly, at the beginning of the GAM programme the relationship aspect is more likely to contribute less than the product/service vehicle. Over time as the GAM relationship strengthens, the relationship aspect will heavily influence and at times determine the product/service aspect. A GAM-related product or service is a vehicle intended to provide a resulting experience that fulfils the client company's global relevant business objectives. It is these experiences that are important to the customer. Through the GAM relationship, the supplying company is in a much better position to understand and deliver a value proposition that meets the needs of the customer's intended results.

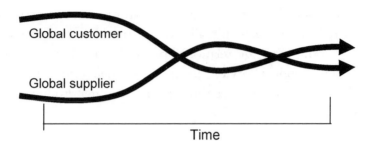

Figure 6.8 The long-term GAM relationship

One example is that of a global account manager serving a global chemical conglomerate who knew more about his client's global operations than those of its diverse business units located around the world. He eventually grew the relationship to a point where he was the important information medium among the business units. Because of his frequent travel among the global chemical conglomerate's business units around the world, he grew to know each business unit's management better than they knew each other and became a key information source for coordinating some of the company's global initiatives. Business units would contact him to obtain strategic and operational information on the company's global business.

Managing the logistics

The logistics vehicle in delivering the GAM value proposition is the distribution network and fulfilment process used to make the product/ service and relationship vehicle accessible to the client company. This includes all the details involved in sourcing, developing, manufacturing and deploying to the client company the product/ service and relationship vehicles. Two aspects to which close attention should be paid in regard to the logistics vehicle are the complexities of the client's global distribution needs and its varying customization requirements.

Managing the communications

The communications vehicle is the means by which a certain client company comes to understand and believe the value proposition. This can be in the form of advertising, presentations, packaging or newsletters, but the most compelling communications vehicle is carried out through the GAM relationship. The global account manager should be continuously communicating the value proposition to the client company.

The following case study illustrates the four vehicles of delivering the value proposition in a GAM programme: relationship, product/service, logistics and communications.

3M/IBM example

3M's IBM global account manager was assigned to manage the IBM Storage relationship (Sperry, 2000). IBM Storage makes giant magnetic resistive (GMR) heads for computer hard drives. The first task that the global account manager assumed was to develop high-level relationships inside the account in order to understand IBM Storage's strategic and operational challenges. The global account manager established multiple relationships, from executive VP to procurement, at IBM Storage's design centers in San José, CA, and Fujisawa, Japan, and at IBM corporate in New York. After a number of months of interviewing, listening and planning, the global account manager began to understand how IBM Storage fitted into IBM's global marketing strategy and observed some of the challenges that IBM faced in manufacturing GMR heads.

3M's IBM account manager also developed relationships at the operational level and worked closely with IBM's design and manufacturing teams. Through these relationships, the account manager was told that one of IBM Storage's major business problems was a manufacturing process that created a disproportionate share of IBM's costs. GMR heads are extremely sensitive to the electrostatic discharge (ESD) created during the manufacturing process. ESD product failures can result in significant product loss.

Knowing that 3M had proprietary technology that could help address IBM Storage's ESD problem, the account manager brought in a core group of four people from 3M's Technology Group to study and solve the problem. This group spent over two years creating entirely new static-dissipative materials to optimize their performance in the manufacturing of GMR heads. Through these collaborative efforts, 3M reduced IBM Storage's GMR product losses by approximately 10 per cent, which translated into an annual saving of several million dollars for IBM. The account manager coordinated the resources that 3M required during the project at IBM's San José design facility.

IBM then asked 3M to supply it multinationally with the new GMR head manufacturing system components. This was a huge opportunity for 3M, because the IBM account manager's group had recently been formed to address just this type of global customer. 3M's IBM account manager became 3M's IBM global account manager. This new responsibility entailed the global account manager introducing the new 3M-designed manufacturing process components to 3M colleagues in all the countries where IBM was manufacturing GMR heads and training the local 3M sales and technical service personnel responsible for servicing the various IBM Storage design and manufacturing branches. The local 3M sales representatives were enthusiastic to cooperate because the new solution allowed each local sales representative to save the local IBM operation millions per year while increasing their own yearly sales by an average of $500 000.

After 3M's focus on IBM Storage shifted from domestic account management to global account management, sales increased by 300 per cent over two years, generating more than $10 million in incremental revenue. When the IBM executives with whom the global account manager had established relationships saw the results, 3M was well positioned for further global partnering efforts. 3M's sales to IBM Storage were projected to increase by 10–25 per cent, partly through three new collaborating opportunities that the global account manager helped identify.

3M's GMR manufacturing process improvement was so successful in delivering value that IBM Storage began to see the global account manager, and the 15 3M technology organizations represented, as critical resources and strategic partners, particularly in customized production problems. When IBM Storage had a problem, it came to 3M's IBM global account manager in the early design stages to see if 3M's resources could help. 3M found itself modifying some of its existing products or combining existing technologies to create new products to support IBM's needs.

Thus in terms of vehicles for delivering the value proposition, 3M's IBM global account manager first developed relationships with individuals and groups throughout IBM Storage's global locations and IBM corporate in order to understand IBM's strategic and operational challenges and global marketing strategy. This relationship development gave the global account manager insight into IBM's culture, how IBM Storage fitted with IBM's overall business strategy and culture, IBM's challenges in manufacturing GMR heads and the opportunity to get to know and build trust with IBM personnel. These relationships resulted in the global account manager being able to distinguish where 3M could most effectively deliver value and establish the credibility and trust to do so.

The relationship cultivated by the global account manager set the foundation for the strategic partnership between 3M and IBM that resulted in new materials that optimized the manufacturing of GMR heads. The resulting product's attributes and its sequential global delivery were a realization of the product/service vehicle in delivering the GAM value proposition because the outcome was profitable for both companies. IBM's intended value proposition experience was achieved with a 10 per cent drop in GMR product loss and multimillion-dollar annual savings; 3M saw sales increase by 300 per cent over two years and an increase in yearly sales by local 3M representatives by an average of $500 000 each.

The communication vehicle in delivering the value proposition was achieved in this example through the global account manager interacting and communicating with stakeholders in both IBM and 3M. The global account manager first convinced IBM and 3M to expend resources on a specific value proposition to reduce product loss through decreasing EDS product failures. Then the global account manager spread the success of the initial delivery of the value position through training local 3M representatives to work with their local IBM counterpart on the new manufacturing process. The communication vehicle continued to deliver value for both IBM and 3M because the global account manager sustained communication throughout both companies, continually refining the model.

The logistics vehicle in delivering the value proposition was accomplished through the global account manager being able to coordinate the movement of resources, personnel and information. The global account manager was able to provide the logistics to establish multiple relationships around the globe with executive and operational levels. The account manager was able to bring together and coordinate resources for a specialized group of four people from 3M's Technology Group to study and solve the problem at the IBM design facility in San José over a two-year period. When the product proved to be a success the global account manager provided the logistical means to train local 3M sales and technical service representatives who were responsible for servicing the various IBM Storage design and manufacturing branches around the world.

MEASURING THE RESULTS

The value of a global account management programme varies from company to company. Ultimately, the programme will align and focus resources on the global customer in order to serve its needs better. For example, Lucent Technologies found that its GAM programme increased customer satisfaction, grew revenues and profits, drove its global process improvement platform, and aligned executive support for a set of accounts. The programme also allowed it more quickly to identify synergistic opportunities across the global account footprint and act with greater speed, and enabled executives to have a higher-quality dialogue with global customers (Kieschke, 2001). The payback from a global account management programme will vary greatly depending on the organizational support, the infrastructure support and the quality of the GAM team and account manager.

CONCLUSION

Understanding a global industry, the global logics and the global accounts strategy is a complex process that is contingent on having selected the right global account. If you have selected a global account that is not interested in anything other than getting the lowest worldwide price, all of your analysis could be worthless. In order to do the analysis and determine how to create global value for a customer, a global account manager with the appropriate competencies must be identified and supported by senior management commitment.

The global account manager will assemble a team of other people who serve the global account, called the global account team, to be discussed in Chapter 7. The global account manager and the global account team will offer a value proposition to the global account, which if accepted will support the global account's strategy. Delivery of the value proposition will require excellent coordination and implementation skills. The ongoing process of delivering this value will be supported through continuing communications with the customer and superior management of the customer relationship.

The Global Account Management Team

7

The path that companies followed in starting their international expansion began with indirect exports from their domestic market, which eventually transformed into global operations. This was initially influenced by the lack of growth opportunities that these companies experienced in their home markets. Early on functional, export and international business unit structures were well adapted to handle the sales volume and manage the extended geographic reach. This model reached saturation point when many of these international business units began to fracture under the pressure associated with the high level of coordination and control required by the increasing scale and scope of the diverse international operations.

This led many companies to set up autonomous international business units, which in turn tended to create internal rivalry between domestic operations and business units and international operations and business units. The rivalry was usually based on the diverse business units, domestic and international, clamoring for top management attention and finite resources. This eventually forced the international divisions to fall into a product/business structure and a geographic area structure, often attempting to balance both simultaneously and ending up with a matrix structure that tried to capture the benefits of both configurations. This balancing act usually resulted in crafting an unbalanced matrix that attempted to overcome the problems associated with dual reporting issues and accommodate historical structures.

The complexities created by international expansion require the global account team to understand the intricacies of dotted-line

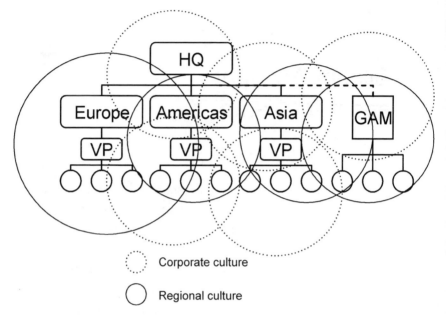

Figure 7.1 Corporate and regional cultures affecting GAM

business relationships, corporate and regional cultures and the varying corporate power bases that the global account management structure must coordinate, as illustrated in Figure 7.1. In order to achieve this within the context of global account management, the proper global systems and processes need to be implemented. This requires companies to adopt a flat, more responsive global structure. The two most important aspects in this transformation in terms of GAM are the global information/communications systems and the global account management team.

A successful GAM programme is the product of numerous inputs, the most important being the team that develops, manages and delivers value to global customers. As mentioned in the previous chapter, the GAM team is essential to the delivery of the global value proposition. The elements that need to be considered when developing and operating a successful GAM team are organizational structure, executive support, internal and external communication, team composition, reporting duties and the global account customer's requirements.

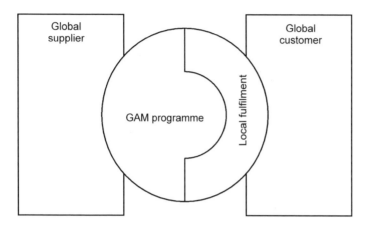

Figure 7.2 Local fulfilment of GAM programmes

One of the most difficult tasks with which the GAM team will be confronted is the reconciling of global strategy with local implementation. The GAM strategy is global, but the tactics and relationship management of the strategy are fulfilled primarily on a local level. This local fulfilment is visualized in Figure 7.2. These factors, combined with regional and corporate cultural influences, create a complex network of relationships in which the GAM team needs to operate.

Research on GAM programmes supports the use of global account managers and global account support staff as being more important than other aspects (Montgomery *et al.*, 1999). The appointment of a GAM manager and support staff is now the most common aspect of GAM programmes. While this is not a surprising finding, it is important because the appointment of a global account manager is almost always accompanied by an organizational change and realignment of responsibilities.

The global customer team is specifically focused on delivering value for the customer. The multifunctional, multicultural team will enhance global value through a better understanding of the customer's strategy. The benefit of the global customer team can be significant. P&G reports that 40–50 per cent of its growth comes from customer teams (Napolitano, 1999).

THE GLOBAL ACCOUNT MANAGER

The global account manager has a key role in constructing the GAM team. This person has primary responsibility for managing the relationship with the global account as well as managing the GAM team around the world. The global account manager position must be more than an elevated sales job. While specific requirements for the position depend on the individual company and its global account, there are some general characteristics and requirements that a global account manager needs to possess.

A global account manager typically has multiple roles both in his or her own company and in the global account organization. The roles identified by Kevin Wilson include boundary-spanning coordinator, entrepreneurial strategist, team leader/manager, politician, information broker, relationship facilitator/builder and negotiator (Wilson, 1999b).

Boundary-spanning coordinator role

The boundary-spanning coordinator role is both internal and external. The internal aspect of a global account manager's role is to be the centre of a network of relationships inside his or her own organization that brings together the necessary people and departments to deliver the global value proposition. This includes bridging the gap between local and global management, between different levels of management, and between different geographic locations and functional specialists. The external aspect of the global account manager's role is to be at the centre of a network of relationships in the global account organization that is as complex as the internal network. This includes contacts with the global account's headquarters executives, global purchasing officers, country managers and local operational people around the world.

Entrepreneurial strategist role

The entrepreneurial strategist role is to identify potential business development and profit creation in the relationship between the supplier organization and the global account. This includes recognizing opportunities to combine the core competencies of the supplier organization and the global account, thus enhancing the global relationship.

Team leader/manager role

The team leader/manager role is to manage and lead in a variety of organizational environments without having direct authority. This requires managing through influence, a responsibility that demands cultural sophistication, empathy, political acumen and developed leadership qualities.

Information broker role

The information broker aspect concerns managing information for the benefit of both the supplier organization and the global account. This requires the global account manager to leverage the relationship networks of which he or she is the centre, in a manner that gleans information valuable to the supplying company's account strategy and the global account.

Relationship facilitator/builder role

The relationship facilitator/builder role is to grow and manage the relationship networks between both organizations. This requires the global account manager to have the ability to manage and build intricate links between the supplier and global account organizations and to monitor the progress of numerous projects simultaneously.

Negotiator role

The negotiator aspect involves both contract and relationship management. The global account manager must be able to establish and administer global agreements and contracts and associated pricing structures. He or she must also be able to reconcile global/ local differences both internally and externally and across business units.

Global account management requires highly qualified global account managers who have the ability to understand key issues and to act quickly in a multitude of cultures, economic environments and business situations. Selection, development and continual improvement of global account managers are the core elements in building and maintaining trusted relationships across diverging cultures, geographies and economies. Global account managers must be able to fully integrate and constantly improve business and negotiating skills with a working knowledge of cultural complexities, international economics and political awareness. They require the political and relationship management skills to influence and manage stakeholders from their own organization as well as the global account's organization without having direct authority.

For example, ING Bank global account managers are required to have years of banking experience, seniority, direct client experience and substantial credit experience. They are also required to have built a personal network within ING that will result in detailed awareness of ING's diversity of people, products and services so that they will be able to facilitate an effective network with clients (Hennessey, 2002).

Citibank's most experienced relationship managers become parent account managers (PAM), Citibank's equivalent of global account managers, of which 95 per cent are recruited internally. The skill requirements for a PAM are team player/networker, international experience, customer needs sensitivity/insight and analysis, counsellor, strategic adviser and problem solver. They must also have influence skills (calling, origination, negotiation), diversity of industry and market knowledge, and be capable of originating structured corporate finance solutions and cross-selling of solutions based on product knowledge. The PAM's career path is managed to develop these skills through specific training programmes and personal development goals linked to evidence of required behaviour (Bowerin, 2000).

The global account manager is the senior point of contact at the customer's headquarters, responsible for marshalling the company's resources to support the customer's requirements, communications and issue resolution. The global account manager position requires a very unique set of skills. Company executives report that it is almost impossible to find someone with all the necessary skills, therefore it is common for companies to appoint global account managers without all the necessary skills who grow into the job and develop through experience and/or training. Schneider Electric, a French electric component manufacturer, has developed global account manager hiring criteria that include the following (Williams, 2001):

- In-depth sales experience.
- Broad knowledge of customers and their industries.
- Broad knowledge of the internal organization, both domestically and internationally.
- A high level of energy and a willingness to travel.
- A thick skin with a tolerance for complexity, difficulty and uncertainty.
- A global business citizen.

Schneider Electric reports that the product mix, process and tools and supply chain complexity make it difficult to hire global account managers from outside the organization. It is easier to find people internally who are interested, but it is still difficult to find those who fit the requirements.

Lucent Technology looks for global account managers with the following abilities (Kieschke, 2001):

- Strong performance in executive leadership and sales skills.
- Major account experience.
- Strong global knowledge and financial acumen.
- Industry and market knowledge.
- Proven ability to work with and through matrix teams.

- Cultural and global openness, including expatriate assignments and language capabilities.
- Comfortable working in ambiguous, unstructured environments.

The Strategic Account Management Association (SAMA) in the US and the Sales Research Trust in the UK conducted a survey of over 200 companies to gain a better understanding of global account management processes and systems. This study identified ten competencies of a global account manager in descending order of importance (Wilson *et al.*, 2000):

- Communication skills.
- Global team leadership and management skills.
- Business and financial acumen.
- Relationship management skills.
- Strategic vision and planning capabilities.
- Problem-solving capabilities.
- Cultural empathy.
- Selling skills, both internal and external.
- Industry and market knowledge of the company and the customer.
- Product/service knowledge.

Similar global account management competencies were reported by PDI Incorporated, Praxair and DHL.

The global account manager as political entrepreneur

Global account managers as political entrepreneurs (Wilson, 2001) primarily perform a boundary-spanning role. They span the boundaries between their own organization and that of the global customer, but they also span boundaries between different functional specialists, geographic locations, departments and levels of management within their own companies. In this respect, they appear at first sight to be very similar to other account managers, but three factors set them apart:

- They tend to forge much stronger and deeper networks of contacts, both at the customer's company and in their own organizations, than do ordinary strategic account managers.
- They often operate under conditions of extreme organizational complexity and cultural diversity. They also tend to be more comfortable with the ambiguity and uncertainties that these conditions create than do their fellow account managers.
- They use their boundary-spanning role quite differently from ordinary account managers in order to focus on the creation of relational value rather than product/service sales.

In addition to the boundary-spanning role, the global account manager when acting as a political entrepreneur is also an analyst, politician, entrepreneurial strategist and global coordinator.

Analysts tend to be team-oriented troubleshooters possessing outstanding knowledge of products/services, technologies and customer industries. Many analysts perceive themselves primarily as international sales managers focusing on global sales targets, sales from regional/national territories and share of customer spending, rather than on opportunities for enhancing levels of value creation and customer profitability.

Politicians combine diplomatic and linguistic skills with cultural empathy and knowledge of global business trends/opportunities. They engage their senior managers in the GAM process and are adept at achieving objectives via influence and persuasion.

Entrepreneurial strategists operate with a fair degree of autonomy. They display high levels of business acumen and look beyond the confines of exchange relationships for business opportunities. They seek out synergistic potential through combining the core competencies of their own organization with those of their global account, even if this requires the formation of new ways of working and organizational entities.

The global coordinator is concerned with coordinating the operational capabilities (manufacturing, logistics, billing, packaging etc.) of the supplier organization to ensure that the customer receives a global offering that also conforms to local demand within a uniform pricing structure, wherever the customer's operations are.

MEMBERS OF THE GLOBAL ACCOUNT MANAGEMENT TEAM

The global account management team typically includes the global account manager, the executive sponsor for the global account, the global customer managers and local service support managers. The size of the team is usually determined by the number of countries, regions and business units serving this global account. GAM teams can range from four or five members to fifteen or twenty.

The global account manager is responsible for leading and coordinating the team. In most cases the global account manager will be located in the country where the global account is headquartered. Occasionally he or she will be located in the country where his or her company is headquartered, in an effort to better coordinate and align company resources to support the global account. The global account manager provides the customer with a single point of contact and access to the supplier's knowledge and expertise. The global account manager should be an expert on the global account's business, its industry, its strategy and its proprietary needs, as discussed in Chapters 3, 4 and 5.

Executive sponsor

The executive sponsor for the global account is the most senior executive in the company responsible for establishing linkages at the highest level of the global customer's organization. The executive sponsor will also help resolve major issues between different geographies and/or different business units that are beyond the scope of the global account manager. Executive sponsors also tend to facilitate access to senior levels of management within the global account. An executive sponsor will normally participate in the account planning process and engage in regular business and social interaction with the customer.

Local account manager

Local account managers are the key sales individuals who call on and service the customer at a local level. Frequently these local account managers will be responsible for geographic regions like Europe or South America. In other cases they will have responsibility for a single country. The main role of the local account manager is to implement the global account strategy on a local basis. This may include delivery of a global product/service offering or tailoring a global offering to the local customer needs.

Another major role of the local account manager is to gather information on local customers' needs, as well as competitive activity. The local account manager is also responsible for resolving operational and logistics problems on a local basis and often oversees the local service support activities and participates in the annual or semi-annual account planning process.

Local service support and other team members

Local service support individuals serve the local needs of the customer. This may include installation activities, maintenance and repair, logistics and supply chain management, and managing technical requirements. Often the GAM team will include a marketing person responsible for key products used by the global customer. The team may also incorporate a product engineer or R&D person to respond to specific customer needs. The composition of the team will vary depending on the needs of the global account.

There are two major aspects of GAM teams, conventional or face to face and virtual. GAM teams frequently utilize characteristics of both conventional and virtual. In conventional terms each team usually has a key group of members, including the global account manager and crucial support personnel, who are located in the same geographic area and are responsible for the overall management of the global account. This key group also meets periodically with the other remote members of the team. This is where the concepts of conventional and virtual intertwine. The global account manager stays in touch with the remote members of the global account team through information technology, creating a virtual team environment.

The virtual team structure adopted by global companies can exist because of the convergence of information and telecommunications technology. This type of team structure allows the global account team continuously to operate 24 hours a day. This could be called a 'following the sunrise' structure of GAM team management. The most difficult aspect of evaluating the global virtual team is that it is a relatively new phenomenon and there is very little empirical evidence concerning global team dynamics and team effectiveness.

Organizational placement of the GAM team

The elements of a GAM team can quickly become complex because GAM programmes and their organizational requirements are superimposed on established organizational structures. Different GAM programmes require diverse organizational changes depending on the supplying company's existing structure and the needs of the corresponding customer base. There is not just one but many ways to organize the teams and the managerial structure for GAM. Each GAM programme will need to organize its team and reporting structures in a fashion that best fits the supplying company and the intended global account customer. This may even result in GAM team structures that will vary within the supplying company depending on the organizational needs of the global customer.

While most global account management structures reflect both the supplier's and customer's organizations, there are also some elements of the structure that are common across all global account management structures. There are several factors concerning a GAM team that are critical to the success of a programme. These include senior corporate-level managers' involvement in continuous and active advocating for the GAM programme and support of the global account team's strategic and operational requirements; the global account manager responsible for leading a global account relationship being provided

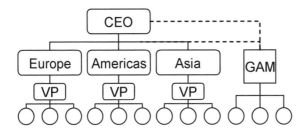

Figure 7.3 Organizational position of GAM

with the tools, access and resources to focus on managing the relationship and the GAM programme; and the GAM team leaders being less than two reporting levels away from the CEO or executive board. This close reporting relationship is illustrated in Figure 7.3.

Positioning the GAM team within an organization is an important aspect of the success of the strategy and team functionality. One of the first issues that arise when implementing the GAM strategy is the location of the GAM teams within the existing organization. Typically, global account management strategies and teams were products of the existing sales and marketing divisions.

However, this organizational structure may create problems as the GAM programme matures and evolves because it needs to be able to coordinate efforts across the company's existing functional silos. Since a primary component of global account management is to break down the internal walls of a company's functional silos, locating global account management in one of the silos has the potential to derail or limit the effectiveness of the programme. One way to solve or avoid this problem is to structure the GAM team in such a way that it transcends a company's corporate functional silos. To accomplish this, the team members should be recruited from different divisions of the company and reflect the direct needs of each individual global account customer.

At Xerox, for example, it is the responsibility of industry-specific SBUs to develop solutions for their particular industries. Within these SBUs are employees knowledgeable in specific industries, some of whom were hired from those industries. Xerox global account management teams leverage this internal industry-specific knowledge to serve their global accounts better (Hennessey, 2002).

Another issue that needs to be addressed is the concept of centralized versus local procurement. GAM teams need to be structured in such a way as to meet the needs of the global customer and its existing internal organizational structure in terms of procurement. Addressing this early on in the adoption of a GAM team is imperative.

If the supplying company does not have the organizational structure to supply globally then the GAM team can be set up outside of existing functional silos. This type of structure can be construed as GAM teams having some sort of global autonomy. The GAM team's autonomy gives team members the ability to service global customers around the world without having constantly to battle the power bases and politics of the company's existing functional silos. In order for teams to be active at this level of global synchronization, there has to be a serious push early on in the adoption of the GAM strategy that brings all the functional silos together to support the programme. This aspect of global alignment was referred to in more detail in Chapter 6. In brief, it is important to remember that effective internal selling of the GAM programme will reduce the political risks created by the global account team's autonomous structure.

Global account management advocate

The global account management advocate should be someone at executive level who absolutely believes in the GAM programme and its future and has the political power and organizational clout to be the final arbiter reconciling internal disputes and moving the programme forward. This position is imperative at the start of a GAM programme and the assembly of the global account team organizational structure. As mentioned before, the start of GAM programmes and the required organizational, strategic and tactical transformations may cause resistance at many different levels of a global business, depending on the organization's legacy reporting hierarchy. If the GAM programme is introduced into an organizational structure that is culturally and managerially decentralized, then the GAM programme advocate should be capable of balancing the team's transition and local internal interests.

The GAM programme advocate should also be able to facilitate communication and acceptance of the programme and its related structural changes throughout the supplying company's various business units, departments and divisions. This will ultimately be followed by the GAM programme advocate going beyond the communication and acceptance stage to facilitating cross-departmental cooperation for the GAM programme and team structure and operations. The GAM programme advocate should also be in a position to promote the programme and team with its global customers. If the GAM programme advocate is of a sufficiently senior position, then the program and team will have a better chance of navigating through the global account selection process.

Resources for the GAM team

The global account manager charged with leading a global account relationship should be provided with the tools, management access and resources to focus on managing the relationship and the GAM programme. The global account manager and the related team should have a fair amount of global autonomy. This means that the lead global account manager and the related key members of the team should have the resources and organizational support to develop the relationship with the global account customer. This sometimes requires significant organizational, strategic and tactical transformation.

A global account steering committee is one effective mechanism by which to achieve this transformation. This committee is most successful if it is made up of senior executives and lead global account managers committed to the GAM programme and capable of resolving the difficulties of global distribution and accounting of resources for the GAM team and reconciling internal cultural, political and economic interests between local interests and the team. The steering committee should also set the strategic direction for the entire GAM programme within the supplying company and make sure that all the company's regional and country managers cooperate on and facilitate the success and progress of the GAM programme and its related teams. Even though the steering committee has responsibility for setting and monitoring the supplying company's overall GAM programme, each specific global account team and its managers should have the responsibly for the strategic direction of the relationship they are charged with managing.

Each individual account team should have the ability and means to develop the specific strategic direction and value proposition for the global account they are charged with managing. This necessitates the teams drawing up an account plan, setting business goals, determining global resource requirements and developing the business relationship with its global account that best realizes the global value proposition, as illustrated in Figure 7.4. The greatest challenge for the GAM team is balancing and managing its specific global organizational mandate with the local company's local stakeholders in such a way that best delivers the value proposition for the global customer. This requires the team to comprise members from different functions of the supplying company, to represent regional cultures that are relevant to the global account's business and to have, as a whole, a diverse and detailed understanding of the culture and organization of the global account customer and its business.

A global account team leader should be no more than two reporting levels away from the company's CEO or executive board. He or she must accomplish two important reporting and perception functions, one internal and one external. The internal aspect of the reporting responsibility provides the GAM programme and individual global account teams with the importance of an executive mandate. This lends the perception that the programme and teams should be taken seriously by the rest of the supplier company. The external aspect of the senior reporting position of a GAM team leader is that the global customer knows for sure that they are being taken seriously and are extremely important to the supplier company. This helps to ensure that inter-company global relationships are primarily built at the

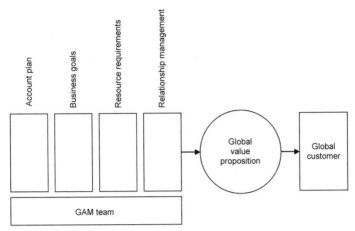

Figure 7.4 GAM management process

executive level, inevitably leading to the GAM programme's value proposition and relationship requirements being taken seriously among varying stakeholders within the global account customer.

Global account management needs to be initiated and managed at the highest level possible, as demonstrated by the organizational chart in Figure 7.5. GAM programmes are expensive and time consuming to implement and senior management involvement helps ensure that necessary resources will be available during the political and cultural turmoil inherent in implementation. Senior management involvement in the long-term GAM process demonstrates to the company's global accounts that the programme is taken seriously and thus facilitates the building of trust.

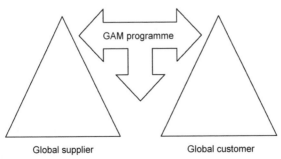

Figure 7.5 Level of GAM interface

The following examples illustrate the importance of senior management commitment to GAM programmes (Hennessey, 2002):

- At Maersk Sealand, each global account has an assigned executive sponsor. Everyone from the vice-president level on up is assigned to be an executive sponsor of a global account.
- All of IBM's global account managers, called client executives, are at the executive level. The client executive in charge of a global account team is made accountable for the account's global revenue, and is responsible for understanding the account's needs and opportunities.
- Steelcase's global account managers are no more than two reporting levels below the vice-president of global accounts.
- At Grey Global Group, the global account manager reports to either the chairman or the president of the company.

The GAM team members should have experience and skills directly relevant to the needs of the global account. They should have broad experience in multiple functions, including operations, management, sales, marketing and relationship management, with specific knowledge of the global account company and the industry in which it operates. Team members should be well versed in how the account operates as a company, understand its culture, know what to expect and how to synthesize this information to ensure value creation. This is illustrated in Figure 7.6.

Manufacturing conglomerate Henkel uses its positioning analysis of its accounts to select a multifunctional team for managing each account. Depending on the results of the positioning analysis, some account teams may be comprised of people strong in marketing, promotion and category management, while other teams will have members strong in accounting and finance (McCann & Hennessey, 2002a).

A majority of logistics company Fritz's global account teams have a background in operations, a primary concern of their accounts. This operations background gives global account managers the ability to

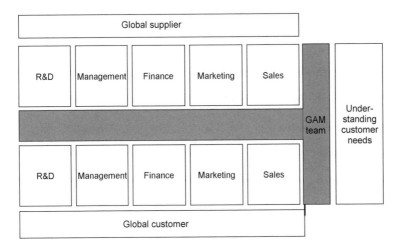

Figure 7.6 Understanding the global customer

change processes, answer questions directly and immediately review issues that arise (McCann & Hennessey, 2002a).

There is a fine line between complete relativism and absolutism when discussing the GAM team's structure and responsibilities. Either approach to the discussion leaves out critical points of the other. Since GAM is a strategic organizational approach around individual customers, each GAM programme and its related teams will have unique aspects. With this in mind, there are critical success factors that are constant throughout GAM in general. As the organizational and cultural aspects of globalization become more familiar in a company or industry, it should be expected that the organizational and structural elements of GAM will evolve and adapt. It is also to be anticipated that the organizational and structural elements of GAM will evolve and adapt to meet continuous changes in the global economy.

MANAGING MULTIPLE CULTURES

Multi-level cross-cultural collaboration is required in a GAM programme to unlock and create value for companies both internally and externally. Global companies typically create influential corporate cultures. Within one corporate culture, there may exist many variations of sub-cultures.

A successful GAM team will need to accommodate the multiple cultures of the team members as well as those of the customer organization. The culture of a country reflects its values, beliefs, customs and behaviour. In the business environment culture is represented by work patterns, office layout, ways of handling disagreements, interactions between leaders and subordinates, communication styles and after-work socialization.

The benefit of cultural diversity lies in the firm's ability to tap into the creativity, knowledge and experimentation that exists within it. The global account manager often assumes the role of cultural orchestrator, as the role spans geography, functions and businesses. Cross-cultural understanding can help facilitate the work of the GAM team. Cultural context research shows that there are low-context countries, such as the US, UK and Sweden, where individuals tend to move directly to work, emphasizing efficiency, specialized skills and performance. High-context cultures, like Brazil, Egypt and India, tend to conduct business in a slow and deliberate way, with a reliance on contextual cues. Trust, goodwill and personal relationships are much more important in high-context cultures (Hall, 1976).

Detailed studies of IBM managers around the world by Geert Hofstede identified four basic cultural dimensions. The first dimension is individualism versus collectivism. In a collectivist society, the identity or worth of people as part of a social system outweighs their value as individuals. The second dimension is small versus large power distance. Large power distance cultures are more authoritarian, with subordinates dependent on bosses. The third dimension is masculinity versus femininity, which reflects cultures dominated by males versus females. The last cultural dimension is weak versus strong uncertainty avoidance, which is a measure of risk tolerance versus risk aversion.

Typically, Venezuelans and Singaporeans are collective and authoritarian, so their behavior tends to be for the good of society and follow the authority of superiors. This situation is the diametric opposite of Americans or Australians, who are individualistic with a small power distance or more democratic. In the uncertainty avoidance and male/female dimensions, Americans, Australians and Venezuelans are all members of masculine cultures, whereas Singaporeans are members of more feminine cultures. In addition, Singaporeans are much more risk tolerant than are Americans or Australians, and much more so than are Venezuelans. Hofstede's analysis provides an overview of cultural differences that helps illustrate national consumer and managerial differences (Hofstede, 1991).

Xerox has identified cross-cultural skills as one of the required competencies of GAM team members. It conducts cross-cultural training for team members to accelerate their cultural understanding.

Global account management can create most value through thinning internal cultural silos and melding internal cross-cultural strengths. Teams with effective cross-cultural collaboration and communication skills can become highly valuable through the individual team members supporting each other by acting as cultural interpreters and mediators. This manner of cultural teamwork becomes highly effective when the team is in the process of executing the GAM strategy locally, for both internal stakeholders and local customer personnel.

For example, advertising agency Grey Global Group is able to spread best practices around the world and quickly coordinate and communicate on behalf of an account. When an advertising campaign is working in one country it is often expanded to many countries, saving the account money and achieving marketing efficiencies for the company and the account (Hennessey, 2002).

De La Rue, a worldwide provider of currency and identity documents, experiences significant uplift in revenue derived from an account when it addresses the account's business strategies and needs by leveraging opportunities that are cross-divisional and require cross-divisional resources.

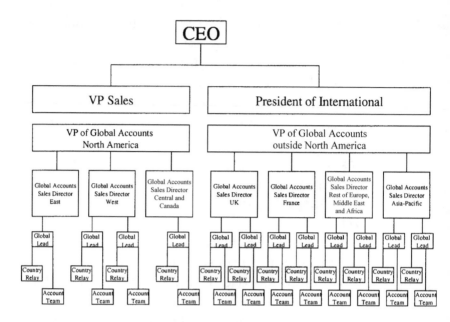

Figure 7.7 GAM organizational structure of office products company

Global office equipment example

Below is an overview of a global office equipment and services company's GAM structure, described in Figure 7.7 (McCann, 2001b):

- *Global account manager (global lead).* This position's responsibilities are global account owner, key relationship owner, integrator worldwide, account advocate, strategist, communicator, coach and teammate and is accountable for sales, account profitability and market share.
- *Global account team member (account team).* This position's responsibilities are to support global initiatives, enhance local market relationships, implement and support global plans on a local level, provide the feedback loop to the account team leader, and have local accountability and communicate with the local customer and dealer.

- *Global account relay (country relay)*. This position's responsibilities are to act as the point of contact between the global team and a local region that deploys support closer to the actual customer's local operations. This is an important position for the business model of this specific global company because actual procurement of its equipment and services is managed through independently operated dealer franchises.

The above structure of a GAM team is one that fits the company's existing cultural and organizational configuration. Since the actual procurement of goods and services is conducted by a local franchise, the three layers in the GAM team support the internal relationship management. The global account manager leads the global account across the globe. The global account team contributes to the strategy and tactics to support the global relationship. The global relay is the local link to the GAM strategy and ensures that the local franchise owners and local corporate employees are positively united with the global teams that are outside their specific geographic area.

An important function of any GAM team is building and maintaining a global network of business relationships and contacts, both formally and informally. The role of networking generally in business-to-business marketing is extremely important and when this is paired with the concepts of GAM opportunities for value creation increase dramatically. The role of networking in regard to a GAM team is fundamental because the basic concept of a GAM programme is to propagate global cross-cultural relationships in order to create value. An important component of the networking role of the GAM team is contact management. The team should have a formal mechanism to identify and record individuals and groups in their own organization and those of customers that have decision-making power and control over resources. It should focus on individuals and groups who have or control access to resources, information, global competencies and influence.

INTERNAL SELLING OF GAM

Implementation of a new GAM programme is a complex process involving numerous people and functions in both the supplier and customer organizations. In a survey of attendees at the SAMA 36th Annual Meeting (Jenni *et al.*, 2002), 44 per cent reported that the biggest obstacle to the implementation of GAM was internal issues/ internal communication, followed by selling issues (17 per cent), customer issues (14 per cent) and administrative issues (14 per cent). The internal selling of GAM is reported to require twice as much effort as its external selling to global accounts. The key reason for resistance to GAM implementation is the threat of a loss of power and authority for local organizations. Regardless of the resistance, the increased demand for global supply, global pricing and global service from customers means that a global programme is necessary or sales on a local level will decline.

Gaining internal support is significantly easier if you select the right people as global account managers. The global account manager needs to have a long-term outlook, collaborate well across the organization and have credibility within the firm. His or her collaborative ability helps build support across organizational units. Credibility increases a person's ability to influence others, even when the global account manager has little or no real authority over others. A common concern for GAM programmes is having enough authority or organizational clout. The organizational structure can either support or hinder the programme. If business unit objectives are aligned with the GAM objectives and supported by appropriate compensation, then in fact the organizational structure gives the global account manager significant authority.

Some firms go one step further and develop alignment plans. These include a description of the global customer's needs, as well as the organizational skills and competencies required to deliver on these needs. The alignment plan also incorporates a statement of the resources and support needed for each business unit or division. The process of developing the alignment plan and getting agreement will facilitate the collaborative effort needed to deliver value to the global customer (Helsing, 1999).

As the global account team will significantly influence the success of the GAM programme, the management of the team is important. Successful teams have a clearly defined mission and clear goals. The team should develop standards covering topics such as how decisions will be made, how conflicts are resolved, and what is handled within the team versus what is handled outside it by the members. Teams also benefit from public as well as individual acknowledgement of their efforts. It is useful to involve team members in customer meetings to build a customer focus. Finally, GAM teams should understand how their individual efforts contribute to the success of the global account. Good team behaviour often includes a process of self-assessment by members (Arnold & Arnold, 2001).

Sika Industry, a division of the Sika Group headquartered in Switzerland, serves the automotive, mass transit, marine, appliances and building industries with sealants, acoustics, flooring and tooling resins. When initially considering a GAM programme, Sika Industry was decentralized worldwide, with no cross-country coordination and a totally local profit and loss responsibility. To understand more about the process of implementing GAM, Sika interviewed customers and internal managers alike on a set of nine variables. These variables focused on three areas with three variables in each area:

- Setting GAM strategy and objectives: customers, solutions, people.
- Aligning organizational structures: relationship, processes, structures.
- Accelerating learning processes: knowledge, systems, information.

The survey of customers and Sika managers helped everyone better understand the areas requiring improvement. A series of workshops were developed to share the results of the survey, define the business drivers, share explicit stories of GAM situations and draw conclusions. These workshops included top corporate management, heads of corporate functions, corporate marketing and local general managers. Their outcome was to show the support of senior management, including the CEO, and gain the acceptance of local country-level management.

The global character of Sika's customers like Volvo, Pilkington, Bombardier, Electrolux, Whirlpool and others required the company to develop a GAM programme. Its top priorities were cross-border project handling to provide the same application and the same solution around the globe, as well as a globally based price.

The following points were learned from the implementation of GAM at Sika Industry (Jenni *et al.*, 2002):

- Open and targeted communication must exist from the very beginning, both internally and to the customer.
- Pragmatic and challenging workshops, internally and with key customers, have a significant impact on the support for the GAM implementation.
- Potential blockages and other obstacles must be identified and involved early in the process.
- GAM is not a project, but rather an ongoing, challenging, yet rewarding process.

Marriott International had 1700 franchises around the world that needed to accept the GAM programme in order to serve 28 alliance accounts globally. As the franchisees normally focused sales and marketing efforts on selling bed nights and meeting rooms in their own hotel, the concept of allowing Marriott International to manage these 28 customers globally was a difficult internal selling job. Marriott gave hundreds of presentations on the new global account initiative, of which over three-quarters were internal presentations to Marriott personnel (McCann & Hennessey, 2002b).

GAM programmes often meet internal resistance. To overcome this, global account managers must develop a team of people to serve the global account, over which the account manager has little or no authority and who are often faced with turf wars. A panel of global account managers from Marriott, Hoffman, Cadence Design Systems and PricewaterhouseCoopers recommended the following to address this situation (Wilson, 1999b):

- Clear definition of global account status.
- Senior management and organizational commitment.
- A structural planning process.
- A process to address threatened entrenched local interests.
- An effective information management system.
- An excellent communication process.

The GAM team is the primary vehicle for delivering the value proposition and it is imperative that it is cognizant of this fact. This requires the team to be knowledgeable and diverse in its make-up, drawing from all departments of the company that are relevant to the customer. The construction of the team, who its members are and its own concept of what a team is should represent more than merely a sales team. Since most strategic and global account programmes stem from a company's sales or marketing function this concept of diversity may clash with the existing business culture of a global corporation. Nevertheless, the GAM team's principal focus is delivering the value proposition through growing the relationship network between two companies. This cannot be accomplished by using members of the corporate sales or marketing function alone. First and foremost, the team should view itself as a business development and relationship builder. The more tactical elements of managing the account and actually booking the sales could be handled by the local or regional sales representatives. This leaves the key members of the global account team to focus on the global business relationship.

A GAM programme can go through several iterations. In other words, there are different levels of sophistication that a company can offer to the customer in regard to global account management. The first one is usually a 'one size fits all' approach. This is when a customer requests, or the supplier company initiates, a GAM programme and the supplying company offers one. The programme that the supplying company offers may at this stage not be very flexible. This can be useful for the inauguration of a GAM programme with a few global customers that are well known to the supplying company.

Solectron has 15 global customer teams generating 75 per cent of total sales. Their success comes from their clear purpose of delivering on the Solectron value proposition. The teams are also cross-functional and cross-business to represent the full value of the company and are led by a seasoned executive. Finally, the teams are driven from the top with direct CEO, presidential and CFO involvement (LaNasa, 2002).

CONCLUSION

The global account management team is responsible for the successful development and implementation of the global account strategy. This team needs to work together to understand the customer's industry, the global logics of that industry and the strategy of the customer to succeed within it. In effect the GAM team becomes a group of consultants that study the situation in detail and attempt to determine as a supplier where they can bring the maximum possible value to the global customer. This needs to be done on a global basis, but also should include the local market needs and the local competitive situation.

To accomplish this task the team needs to have the right global account manager, the right team members and the right level of senior management support and commitment. After the strategy to develop the maximum possible value for the global account is presented and agreed by the customer, the GAM team members must align and coordinate across their own organization to deliver the agreed value. The firm's interpersonal, interorganizational and intercultural skills can either contribute to or block the process.

Supporting and Implementing Global Account Management   8

Many firms that have successfully implemented a global account management programme have found that key success factors include senior management commitment, selecting the right global accounts, selecting appropriate global account managers, creating significant global value for the global account, and alignment of company resources to support the global account strategy. All of these factors have been discussed in Chapters 1–7.

A survey of global account managers in 2001 indicated that the biggest challenges that arise with the implementation of a GAM programme are turf wars between local and global people (68 per cent mentioned), implementation of the strategy on a local level (61 per cent), lack of an integrated information technology system (50 per cent) and managing a multinational team (44 per cent). These challenges need to be addressed for a GAM programme to be successful (Wilson *et al.*, 2000). Supporting the global account programme and its value delivery is the need for an appropriate information technology system, alignment of compensation and metrics, and organizational support to address the conflicts between local and global interests. This chapter will cover these necessary supporting factors.

INFORMATION TECHNOLOGY INFRASTRUCTURE

Global account management cannot operate effectively without a globally integrated information system. This information is required to serve the global account effectively. First, global revenues need to be tracked by account, to determine which accounts are the largest. While this seems like an easy task, firms often have different information systems in different countries, which are difficult to merge. In addition, customers have different names in different countries or, in some cases, the revenues may be attributed to a subcontractor or another firm. In one case it took three months for a multibillion-dollar computer firm to identify its top 100 customers. The task was eventually accomplished manually.

Secondly, to understand a customer it is critical to know what products it is using in which countries. Third, to assess the opportunities to serve the account better globally it is necessary to have adequate, up-to-the-minute information on all account interactions, including sales, shipments, returns, technical meetings, sales calls, executive meetings and so on. This can only be accomplished with a sophisticated global information system.

Knowledge management

The establishment of a GAM programme requires a system that includes all information on a global account. The information systems infrastructure facilitates easy access to and communication of internal information on sales, returns, inventory, sales calls, technical problems and so on from a disparate group of people around the world. The global account manager and global account team need to aggregate and analyse this information. This global aggregation of information is illustrated in Figure 8.1.

While the information is important, often the critical component of know-how is not captured in an information management system. For example, an increase in sales of polyurethane in Indonesia showed up in a supplier's monthly sales numbers. In this case the supplier's application engineer was able to increase throughput with a new blending method. Therefore the customer's switch brought additional volume to the firm, but the technical solution that the engineer developed may not show up for others in the company to

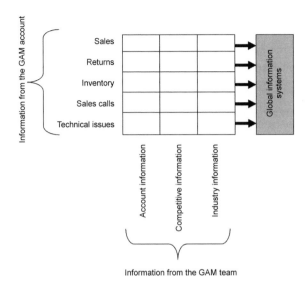

Figure 8.1 Global aggregation of account information

copy. Know-how is often difficult to formulate and transfer in any systematic way.

The challenge of any global account management system is to be able to collect this type of local know-how that accumulates every day as employees solve routine customer problems. The know-how is held by employees and is either lost or transferred through success stories in informal meetings with peers. Without the transfer of this know-how, other employees must reinvent solutions to the same problems over and over again. The transfer of local know-how is illustrated in Figure 8.2.

The global account manager represents the firm to the global customer and is expected to know all the products and services being used by the customer, all joint programmes and projects, and all problems between the two firms. This is the minimum standard in order to have credibility with the customer. In addition, the global account manager must have a strategic understanding of the customer's future needs. Based on this view of the future, the supplier must ask how it can best add value to help support the customer's strategy.

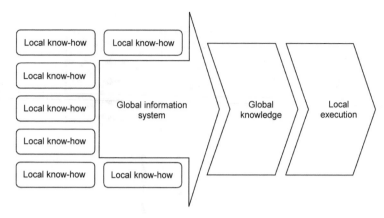

Figure 8.2 Development of global knowledge

Much of this strategic view will come out of the global account team's study of the customer's industry and strategy. This centralized view is important, but does not replace local knowledge of the customer based on years of experience and long-term relationships.

It is critical for best practices and success stories to be shared, so that where appropriate they can be standardized and leveraged across the global account. The ability to leverage knowledge from 30, 50 or 100 countries often provides the insight needed to create real global value. Lew Platt, former CEO of Hewlett-Packard, said: 'I wish I knew what HP knows.' HP's global account management programme is supported by the Electronic Sales Partner (ESP) platform. ESP allows sales representatives to sign in and ask questions on certain topics. This search engine allows easy access to worldwide HP solutions, presentations, contracts and other documents. Each global account team has its own site with links to the customer's web page, new releases on the customer, relevant HP research on the customer and other customer-related information (Arnold *et al.*, 2001).

Research based on a survey of 101 executives with GAM experience found that developing a process to manage knowledge exchange has a direct positive impact on global accounts. Knowledge exchange increased global account satisfaction, the amount of innovation at global accounts and the penetration of global accounts through a wider range of products and services. Knowledge exchange contributes directly to the success of a GAM programme, as measured by growth in sales volume and share of the account's business. The same study of GAM executives showed that the variables facilitating knowledge exchange are (Arnold *et al.*, 2001):

- A good information technology system.
- Establishing the GAM programme as a profit centre.
- Having clear processes that allocate responsibilities between the global account manager and local management.
- Public acknowledgement of the GAM programme.
- A strong group identity for the GAM programme.

Oracle example

Oracle identified 185 strategic accounts out of 100 000 customers. Feedback from these multi-country strategic accounts was that Oracle was difficult to do business with on a global basis. It therefore developed a global account management programme information system and launched a GAM programme. The revenues from global accounts were 15–20 per cent higher than other Oracle accounts. Oracle's global customers benefited from the GAM programme because they were able to deal with a single person who had full global responsibility, could leverage their global buying power, facilitate global standards and leverage local implementation successes on a global basis (NAMA, 1998).

Customer relationship management (CRM)

Global accounts want to be served by a unified, organized, integrated supplier. The global customer does not want the transactional costs or inconvenience of interacting with a supplier's various lines of business or different geographies acting as uninformed silos. Global customers will partner with a limited number of strategic core suppliers. This means that a core supplier will become part of the customer's global extended enterprise.

Many organizations have invested millions of dollars in CRM systems, although with mixed results. The investments in CRM offer the opportunity to greatly improve the relationship with global customers by virtue of the additional information available to the global account team. According to a survey of sales managers, IT managers and CRM implementation managers in Fortune 500 companies, many current CRM systems are overloaded with transactional information, but the information does not provide a strategic view of the account. The survey also found that CRM systems tend to be focused on internal processes with little or no customer feedback or input.

The CRM system needs to be more than a warehouse of information. It should provide analysis of the data with a strategic perspective. In addition, CRM needs to include the customer's input. For example, customer complaints that come through a call centre or service centre are often not included in a CRM system. Direct feedback from the customer could also be added to the system (Gadnis, 1999). Finally, strategic information on the customer's industry and strategy should be included in the CRM. This new, expanded view of the customer will be helpful to product development and engineering as well. When CRM becomes web enabled, it may be possible to share this relationship information with global customers to support a seamless partnership.

Marriott's CEO sponsored a taskforce to analyse the deployment of its salesforce. The result was the Sales Transformation Program, which moved the sales effort from a product orientation to a customer orientation. To support this, Marriott invested $25 million in a Siebel CRM system. Its Strategic Accounts Division is now able to track the global company's use and satisfaction. While Marriott was historically a strong business-to-consumer organization, recognizing the high-volume traveller, it is now focused on recognizing and supporting its large global customers. For example, it has appointed a global account manager for IBM, who directs a sales team of 70 people to manage local relationships. Along with executive sponsorship and a change in organizational structure, the CRM system supports major cultural change at Marriott (Gartner Group, 2001).

ALIGNMENT OF COMPENSATION AND METRICS

Compensation of global account team members can be difficult because salaries must be high enough to attract people with the required unique competencies. The salaries must also be in line with those of the geographic area where the global account manager is located. If the GAM team's salaries are too high, it may affect other executives who perceive their role to be of equal or greater importance.

A group of seven companies participating in The Global Forum of the Strategic Account Management Association (Dun & Bradstreet, IBM, Cable & Wireless, Reuters, Xerox, ABB and Young & Rubicam) recommend that a GAM programme should include some compensation tied to global sales and/or profit of the global account. Dun & Bradstreet Global reported that its global customer manager's (GCM) compensation was tied to the global performance of the account. The compensation was in line with other D&B employees in the country in which the GCM was located. D&B also included incentives for other managers in the GCM's chain of command to assure their support (SAMA, 1999).

Developing a compensation plan for global account managers is challenging because the participants tend to be located around the world, with limited comparable data. Generally, global account managers tend to have a greater portion of their salary fixed and less of it variable compared to traditional sales representatives. This is because a global account manager role typically has a longer time horizon than that of a traditional salesperson.

IBM has a global compensation system that seeks to maintain consistency for global account teams. Global client executives are paid a salary plus a bonus based on the global results of the client. The management team sets the global targets. The global client executive sets the targets for remote team members. The management team is paid on the global results, meaning the performance of the global client executive (Uittendroek, 2000).

It is a common practice to provide the GAM team with some commission or bonus based on the global account sales volume, although this can lead to conflicts with local salespeople and sales managers who also feel responsible for sales results. In some firms revenues are double counted, once for the local sales team and once for the GAM team, with commissions or bonuses awarded to both (Croom *et al.*, 1999).

The survey data indicates that global account manager compensation plans tend to include revenue and profit measures, as well as a measure of the sales process and account plan development. In general, out of a total of 100 per cent, sales results comprise 55 per cent, while profit results are 35 per cent and sales process measures are 25 per cent.

The total compensation paid to global account managers varies by industry. As shown in Table 8.1, the total compensation in 2000 for global account managers was consistently higher than that for national account managers.

As the data indicates, global account managers receive higher pay than national account managers. When setting global compensation levels, it is important to benchmark with syndicated sales surveys, association surveys, the Strategic Account Management Association

Table 8.1 Total compensation for global and national account managers by industry

	Global (N=81)	National (N=175)
Other services	$121 348	$112 414
Chemicals	$122 298	$117 997
Other manufacturing	$138 875	$115 905
Telecommunication	$165 000	$99 460
High technology	$285 022	$124 208

Source: Scott, Elliot & Ingalls, Gidgett (2001) 'Leading edge compensation design for strategic account management programs', *Strategic Account Management Association Annual Conference*, May, pp. 1–56.

	VP Sales	Global Accounts Director	Global Account Manager	Regional Sales Director	Salesperson Senior	Salesperson Junior
Sales volume						
Profit						
New accounts						
New products						
Price realization						
Product mix						
Account growth						
Total compensation						
Base						
Incentive						

Figure 8.3 Framework for analysing the workload and responsibility of sales positions

(www.strategicaccounts.org), consultants or through your own benchmarking system. While benchmarking global account managers' compensation is important to ensure that managers are being paid an externally competitive compensation, sometimes internal comparisons are equally important. The global manager's compensation should be appropriate relative to other sales positions. It is useful to compare the workload and responsibilities of various sales positions in the firm to confirm that compensation and responsibility are aligned. Figure 8.3 gives a framework for these comparisons.

Evaluating all of these positions in terms of their responsibilities, level of influence and complexity helps to align job measures and compensation levels properly.

A survey of 81 global account managers found that their compensation programmes had an average of three criteria for the variable portion of the compensation (Scott & Ingalls, 2001). The leading criteria to be used to determine the variable portion of global account managers' compensation are shown in Figure 8.4.

Selecting the right measures is difficult as the role of the global account manager is multi-faceted and the link between short-term sales and the global account manager is weak. In addition, long sales and buying cycles make measurements difficult.

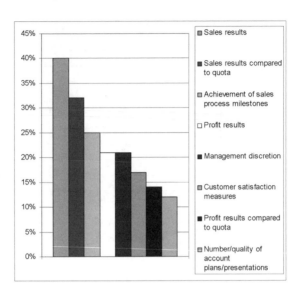

Figure 8.4 Criteria for determining the variable portion of global account managers' compensation

Another difficulty with global account managers' compensation levels is their inclusion as part of the GAM team. Global account managers are often on teams with local account managers, service managers and other managers serving the global account. The success of global account managers requires effort from local sales and service representatives, who receive compensation based on local country results, not global results. This sharing of responsibility often causes firms either to split or double count the revenue or profit credit for compensation.

Global compensation systems face a number of environmental variables. The local compensation design may not support the complexity of multinational sales efforts. Buyers and buying influences are increasingly located in multiple countries. Different countries have different work hours and compensation requirements. They also have different tax structures and levels, as well as a different cultural acceptance of incentive compensation.

There is resistance to using incentive plans that tie compensation to performance, especially in Japan. However, GE Financial Services, PCA Japan and Global, an insurance firm, all adopted sales compensation plans linking salary to performance. These firms all attracted and retained very successful salespeople. This indicates that the reluctance of many Asian and European companies to put a significant portion of compensation at risk may be incorrect (Blessington & Sands, 2002).

To assess how much of a global account manager's compensation should be tied to volume objectives, it is important to understand the global account manager's ability to influence results. Does he or she have full responsibility for all products at the global account? Does he or she have authority over the various divisions and product lines selling to the account? What is the primary objective of the global account manager: to grow revenue, to grow share, or to develop the relationship?

Schneider Electric has developed a compensation programme that includes 75 per cent base salary and 25 per cent bonus. The bonus is weighted 50 per cent based on sales of the global accounts, 10 per cent on achieving account plans, 10 per cent on the quality of the account relationship, 10 per cent on programme implementation, 10 per cent at the sales director's discretion, and 10 per cent at the international account manager's discretion (Williams, 2001).

ORGANIZATIONAL SUPPORT

ABB was created in 1988 through the merger of BBC Brown Boveri of Switzerland with ASEA of Sweden. The firm was organized by segments and business areas to service its clients. In 1993 it began a pilot for a global account management programme to serve selected globally oriented clients. The global key account manager had a dotted-line responsibility to ABB's Executive Committee.

Dr Fritschi was the global account manager in fine chemicals and pharmaceuticals. He had very close contact with the headquarters of three companies in Basel, Switzerland. Through his relationship with senior executives, he learned very early about plant expansions or renewal plans. While the typical ABB client would now know about all ABB businesses, the global account manager can help the client tap into ABB's resources. Revenues of ABB's fine chemical/ pharmaceutical business grew by 150 per cent from 1993 to 1998, while the industry average was only 10 per cent (Fritschi, 1999).

Metrics can have a big influence on behaviour. Logistics group Fritz had 43 different distribution centres, all with their own P&L statements. It was not surprising that if a global customer was less profitable for a specific distribution centre, the customer would not get the required level of service. Fritz decided to create 25 separate P&L statements for its global customers. The global view of these important customers helped the local distribution centres see the need for a consistently high level of customer service, regardless of profitability at the local level. Fritz moved its divisions to new metrics of customer service, quality and productivity goals. This resulted in higher customer satisfaction and increased profitability (McCann, 2001d).

Management processes

Global account management is a management process that influences other management processes. The global account manager will accumulate all the information on an account through the company information systems. This global view of the customer will help coordinate the local country interactions with the customer. The global account manager will influence the budgeting process to align company resources to support the account. He or she will also assemble information on the global performance of the account that could affect compensation practices.

People

Global account management needs people who can take a global view of the customer. These global account managers will be interacting with others in the company who will have to understand the global perspective. Managers who normally worry about customer actions in a single country like Germany must understand why the customer is moving facilities to Brazil or China. This requirement for more managers with a global mindset is critical to the success of a GAM programme. The development and implementation of a GAM programme involves changes in four significant organizational areas (Yip & Madsen, 1996):

- The organizational structure of who reports to whom.
- Management processes, including activities of budgeting, planning and information systems, which together help run the business.
- People, who comprise the human resource of managers and employees.
- Culture, which comprises the values and rules guiding behaviour in a company.

Organizational structure

When creating the position of global account manager, the company needs to determine to whom the position will report and what authority the position will have. If the global account manager reports to a director of global accounts, who reports to the vice-president of sales, the role will be perceived differently than if the global account manager reports directly to the CEO. The global account manager will have some degree of authority over local operations. This can vary from direct control to coordination to advice. In many cases, the global account manager will coordinate the activities of the local account manager without having direct control.

Culture

The company's culture can play a significant role in the success or failure of a GAM programme. As a company develops its global perspective, it will shift from local profit maximization to global profit maximization. Global account management often causes a firm to confront the reality that customers have become global and that it must follow customers geographically and culturally (Yip & Madsen, 1996).

Training and education

Given the nature of the role that global account management plays, it is difficult to identify a large number of people who possess all the relevant skills. Many of the skills associated with a general manager would benefit someone working on a global account. These include strategic skills, analytical skills, leadership skills and an ability to understand financial performance. The skills of a key or national account manager would also be useful for individuals working with global accounts. These include communication skills, selling and negotiation skills, relationship management, team management skills and the ability to work across different products and services.

In addition to these skills, individuals working with global accounts must be able to handle organizational complexity. This complexity includes multiple business units, multiple hierarchical levels and multiple geographies. On top of all these skills, those serving global accounts must be able to thrive in a multicultural environment. This requires not only an understanding of a variety of different national cultures, but an idea of how to facilitate the interaction of multiple cultures.

Given all of the skills and competencies required, it is not surprising that there are few individuals with all the necessary qualifications. It is very unusual to recruit a global account manager from outside the company. Most global account managers come from inside, therefore they have the benefit of understanding the company's culture, products, services and the formal and informal network. Often the size of the global account management programme is limited by the number of qualified account managers.

Most companies with global account management programmes have an education programme. For example, DSM Engineering Plastics launched a GAM programme in 1999 to serve large customers in electronics, automotives and telecommunications. To launch the programme, the executive sponsor held a one-week training programme for the global account teams. This was conducted at a leading business in the US, where the teams were exposed to the process of industry analysis, strategy formulation and value creation. The teams worked on their global account and at the end of the week presented an analysis of the account and an account plan to create value to support the global accounts strategy. These presentations were given to three or four members of division management.

IBM has a number of initiatives to support global account management. The client executives attend a programme at a major university that uses case studies to build their consultative selling skills. Global client executives are given education on the global aspects of GAM, such as cultural sensitivities, building global relationships and understanding global trends. IBM also has ongoing education for its global teams. This includes marketing to international clients, global contracts and international project management (Uittendroek, 2000).

Xerox found that it needed to develop cross-cultural training for global account managers. A workshop conducted by Xerox managers was held in different parts of the world on topics such as how different cultures handle conflict, respond to time concerns, respond to status or balance individual needs versus community needs. The seminars helped global account managers gain a better understanding of the multicultural dimension (McCann & Hennessey, 2002a).

Van Leer Industrial Packaging established a global coordinator position to help serve global accounts. After the loss of a large contract for TOTAL, a French oil company, the senior executive responsible for industrial packaging held an executive programme at a well-known European university. In addition to people directly serving global accounts, he also invited the country sales managers and country managers. The programme used cases to explore the process of managing global accounts, including a case series written on Van Leer's loss of the TOTAL business. The seminar helped educate the division managers on the importance of global accounts and the need to work cooperatively to serve them (Weinstein, 1998).

MANAGING THE CHANGE TO GAM

Siemens, a 150-year-old German company with $70 billion in sales and 400 000 employees, found that the development and implementation of a global account management programme required a number of significant changes. Given that Siemens had a very decentralized sales structure that focused on the regions and the country leaders in charge of their area with separate P&L statements, it was difficult to offer global customers seamless products and services. When Coca-Cola approached Siemens in 1991 and asked to be supplied with products and services throughout Europe and Asia, Siemens saw this as a catalyst to set up a global partnership with one of its largest customers.

It selected Citibank, Coca-Cola, Dow and IBM for global partnership agreements. A global umbrella agreement with Coca-Cola became a template for global accounts, as well as a process to change the Siemens organization. The global partnership agreement included rules of engagement, a global strategy for the account and changes that the customer required from Siemens in order to agree to the partnership.

Siemens was able to facilitate the cultural change through a series of process change mechanisms. First, international account managers received a percentage of any sales made to the global account anywhere in the world. This ensured that the global account manager would support any business opportunity and not focus only on the domestic market. Second, Siemens established a network of contacts in 80 countries who could be contacted by the global sales team to service issues locally for global customers. Third, the Siemens global account team had to obtain approval from the business units and divisions for their account plan. The divisions would allocate funds to the global account team to sell the division's products. If the plans were successful, the global account team would receive more funds.

Fourth, Siemens established an international account forum that was sponsored by a senior executive and met regularly. This group comprised contact managers from 80 countries who serviced global accounts. The forum identified problems and recommended changes to serve global customers better. Finally, Siemens required all global account team members to undergo intercultural training. It believed that to be successful with an account, you needed to interact with the customer based on gaining significant knowledge of its country's culture. According to David Macaulay, Siemens' Senior Vice-President of Global Accounts, 'One of the keys to our global success has been our acceptance of different cultures. If you don't understand culture or are not sensitive to another person's culture, doing business can be twice as hard' (Macaulay, 2001).

MANAGING CONFLICT BETWEEN GLOBAL/LOCAL INTERESTS

The organizational structure for large companies in multiple countries is often a country-based profit structure. This means that local managers are measured and rewarded based on their country's sales and profit. This reporting structure allows local management to focus on increasing sales while maintaining or reducing costs.

When attempts are made to overlay a global account management programme with a country-based organization, there is natural tension. Local management is measured on local sales, not sales to other countries. So while a local engineer may be needed to explain technical specifications to an applications engineer at the customer's headquarters for materials to be used in another country, the local manager would prefer to focus this resource on local sales. Often the global account manager is carried on the country's P&L statement, which can be a problem because the country manager wants the global account manager to focus on local needs, not on needs in other countries. Steelcase found examples where global account managers were told that they could not leave the country as their salaries were paid by the local country.

To overcome the tension caused by a country-based P&L, an executive commitment from senior executives in headquarters or the regions is needed to sponsor the GAM programme. The country manager needs to understand that serving global accounts will support the company, the region and, eventually, his or her country's performance. Senior management support of GAM is critical.

Another way to facilitate proper attention to global accounts is to fund the account's development and growth. Square-D, a subsidiary of Schneider Electric, has developed a 'Seed, Feed and Reap' plan to fund customer development (Williams, 2001). After a global account is selected, the supplier's senior management allocates resources to the appropriate countries to develop the relationships and business. The senior executives will continue to fund the potential account with 'feed' money to support best practice. In the reap phase, the countries that helped develop the business are given sales credit, even if the sales were in another country. As the sales cycle on a major account could take between three and five years, the seed, feed and reap funding programme takes place over many years.

Another global/local tension that arises is the lack of customer centralization of a global account. Some customers are not organized to interact globally, so global suppliers are faced with the challenge of interacting with every local subsidiary. In these cases local support is critical to allow for the potential of a global supplier. In some cases the supplier can help the customer establish global procurement. In other cases it may be better to wait until the customer is ready to examine its global procurement options.

Often local subsidiaries purchase unique specifications that differ from country to country. With product and service offerings varying greatly around the world, it is more challenging to manage the relationship globally. To address the differences from country to country, it is important to understand the company's strategy in each market. Through understanding the gaps, it is possible to deliver a strategy that closes the gaps. It may also be necessary to build channel relationships to meet service gaps in some countries.

Global pricing and contracts

Pricing is a key element in any global account relationship. As global customers develop centralized procurement, they will expect some form of special pricing in exchange for guaranteed volume and improved economies of scale. As the vice-president of global marketing at electronics company AMP said, 'Customers love a vendor's global account management system because, as soon as a global account manager is designated, they see one person whom they can beat to death to get a lower price' (Narayandas *et al.*, 2000). This sums up one of the biggest fears of global suppliers: global pricing.

As customers begin to leverage their global size, there is often a demand for global pricing or global volume discounts. The supplier's local profit margin will fall, again potentially reducing local support. To address this challenge, it is important to understand the relative price that a customer is receiving in each geographic market. While customers realize that manufacturing costs vary from market to market, it is important to offer fair country-based pricing based on local solutions. Schneider Electric recommends the development of a country-based pricing model, which can be developed and tested by the customer to verify fair local pricing.

Global customers around the world have begun to buy on a coordinated basis. Customers see this coordinated purchasing as a way to add value. Global customers have information systems that allow them to track supplier prices, quality and service worldwide. David Macaulay at Siemens comments, 'When you ask customers what their primary requirements of a global supplier are, the most common response is worldwide consistency. This can take the form of consistent pricing, logistics, ease of doing business, advertising, support, implementation, service quality, etc.' (Macaulay, 2001).

Some customers may require global pricing, which of course also demands global product/service standards. However, in most cases global customers understand that costs are different in different countries, therefore allowing for different pricing.

Through customer satisfaction surveys D&B Global found that its global customers were dissatisfied with its pricing approach. They wanted consistent and rational pricing in all locations and for the pricing policy to reflect the company's total commitment to D&B worldwide. To address these customer concerns, D&B had to coordinate and simplify all pricing agreements. For global accounts it developed a global umbrella agreement that supplemented local contracts, providing a consistent discount based on the global volume of the account. D&B also required global accounts to designate it as a preferred supplier, moving the relationship from a transactional basis to a partnership (SAMA, 1999).

As global customers will require some form of global pricing, firms must prepare themselves. Global customers are asking for global pricing contracts. These contracts will exchange guaranteed volumes for an agreed price. The guaranteed volumes should result in economies of scale for the supplier and therefore reduce costs. The supplier should also benefit from joint product development, standardization of product offerings, reduced transaction costs and lower supply chain costs. Suppliers may be able to use global contracts to expand with global customers to new markets and with a predictable stream of business. Global contracts can also be used for marketing purposes to show a firm's strength as a global supplier to IBM or Ford, for example (Narayandas *et al.*, 2000).

Before participating in global pricing negotiations, it is important to have complete information. Information on the customer, its needs and its strategy is critical, as well as information on the costs in various countries. The customer's needs should include order size, frequency and predictability. This information is necessary to determine logistics costs. The local costs of production, logistics, taxes and exchange rates can all contribute to differences that may need to be included in the contract.

The negotiation of global contracts involves a large number of issues beyond the scope of this book. However, the objectives of both the global supplier and the global customer should be aligned to provide maximum value at a reasonable cost. This objective leads to a partnership where two companies can work together to reduce costs while enhancing value.

Supply chain management is an excellent opportunity to reduce costs. For example, compatible systems can allow a customer to check delivery status online, rather than having to speak to a customer service representative. Coordinating sales forecasts and inventory management can reduce safety stock levels, thereby reducing costs. In one case a supplier and a customer who worked together on a single team identified after only two meetings 17 action plans to reduce costs through collaboration by redefining roles and boundaries between the two firms. The savings and improved margins for both firms solidified the partnership (Pope & Brown, 2002).

CONCLUSION

The process of developing and implementing a global account management programme is complicated and involved. The first step is to examine your possible global customers to determine if they would benefit from being served globally by your firm. The second is to develop a deep-seated conviction on the part of senior management that global account management is required. This senior management support is necessary to allocate the resources and implement the change from the current organizational structure to a new structure. At a minimum the global account management structure will be laid over the current structure, resulting in turf wars and trade-off decisions that will require senior management involvement.

The third step in the process is the identification of appropriate global accounts and global account managers. Generally companies serve an average of 8–10 global accounts, but there are examples of global firms with over 100 global accounts. The number of global accounts will influence the cost of the GAM programme. The next step in global account management is the development of a global account plan, which can only be done after an in-depth analysis of the customer's industry, the key success factors in the industry and the customer's strategy to be successful in that industry. This in-depth understanding gives the global supplier the opportunity to identify unique options to deliver value to that specific global customer. Chapters 3–6 focused on the intermediate steps to understand the customer's industry and opportunities to develop value.

This chapter has addressed many of the challenges of implementing a GAM system, such as managing the conflict between the global account manager and the multiple countries or business units, managing the change process from a traditional account management system to a global account management system, aligning compensation systems between all the different parts of the company that serve the customer's needs, and developing the appropriate internal training programme to support the GAM programme. A successful global account management programme will require an appropriate information technology system, a knowledge management process and possibly a customer relationship management programme. Often global accounts also require global contracts and global pricing.

Global account management is relatively new. While a few service companies in accounting, advertising and consulting have been using some form of global account management for years, the bulk of companies with global account management have had it for five years or less. The purpose of this book has been to share the collective learning and wisdom of the firms, consultants and researchers who have experienced the success or failures of global management. In addition, we have shared our own experience of over 20 years in global strategy and global marketing, along with our experience helping firms establish global account management. We expect that as more firms use global account management for competitive advantage as well as to serve global customers more effectively, the practice of global account management will become more sophisticated. The best firms will be those who continually learn new and better ways to create value for their global customers.

Appendix

Global Account Management in Action

Xerox Corporation: Global Account Management

GLOBAL ACCOUNT MANAGEMENT OVERVIEW

Xerox has had a global account management programme for 15 years. In 1986, it started with a global account management test programme for six major accounts. In 1988 the programme was expanded to 12 accounts and then again in 1989 to 24 accounts. Throughout the 1990s, Xerox's global account management programme continued to grow and as of September 2001, the company had 150 global accounts.

Global account managers reside in the home country of their assigned account. That country unit incurs a global account manager's salary and expenses but he or she takes direction from the industry VPs. In Germany, for example, the general manager has eight global account managers reporting to him, including the global account managers for BMW, Volkswagen and Allianz Insurance. These global account managers also report to Xerox's VP of Industrial, in the case of BMW and Volkswagen, or Xerox's VP of Financial Services, in the case of Allianz Insurance. Joint reporting in Europe occurs because global account managers are on the books of

This case was prepared by W. Caleb McCann, MBA, Babson College, and H. David Hennessey, Associate Professor of Marketing and International Business.

This case was drawn from a conversation with David Potter, Director Global Account Field Operations at Xerox Corporation, and from public information sources and written as a basis for class discussion rather than to illustrate either effective or ineffective handling of a business situation.

Xerox's individual country units. In the US, global account managers report to the various industry vice-presidents who are part of the US management team.

Xerox has more than 100 global account managers, each of whom handles one or two accounts. 'Tier 1' accounts have a dedicated global account manager in almost all cases. A few global account managers have other responsibilities, although this is contrary to the design model. For example, the global account manager for a global banking group is also the channel manager for financial services in the Netherlands. The reason for this variance from the design is that 80 per cent of Xerox's business with this global banking group is outside of the Netherlands, so Xerox's Dutch unit wants to spread the cost of a relatively high-powered salesperson over other functions.

SELECTING GLOBAL ACCOUNTS

Xerox has three initial criteria that companies need to meet to become a global account:

- The first criterion is that a potential global account spends at least $10 million a year with Xerox. Tier 1 accounts have global purchases of $15 million and Tier 2 $10 million.
- The second global account criterion is that a potential global account be global in both business practices and organizational structure. Xerox requires global accounts to do business globally, but does not require global purchasing. Some Xerox customers conduct business globally but are locally organized and managed. In this situation, even if the customer spends over $10 million a year with Xerox, there is no strategic benefit to Xerox for dedicating a global account manager to the customer.
- Third, a global account must be willing to collaborate with Xerox. Xerox's global account management programme goes beyond just selling products and works with global accounts to help develop value-added solutions. In order to do this successfully, a global

account needs to share its business issues, key success factors and strategy with Xerox.

Most large customers have multiple brand divisions as well as administration, marketing and other functions. Part of the challenge for global account managers is being able to get their arms around all of the divisions while managing their time efficiently. That is why Xerox wants to ensure that the customer is willing to make an equal investment in the relationship.

Global accounts have global, regional and/or local contracts. This gives Xerox flexibility to build relationships and strategically align with customers who do not meet all the global account criteria but are in the process of building a global strategy. For example, in 1999 Motorola was a Xerox global account but was not able to commit to a global contract. At the time, its only extensive contract with Xerox covered the United States and this contract was not considered truly comprehensive. However, Motorola had a proactive manager running its Asia operation who wanted to leverage its global account relationship with Xerox and not 'wait for those people at headquarters to get their act together'. This resulted in Xerox doing a comprehensive Asia deal with Motorola.

GLOBAL ACCOUNT INFORMATION SYSTEMS

Xerox has a product called Docushare, which is document-sharing groupware. It allows global account managers to set up web pages without having to use HTTP programming. Xerox's global account managers all have web pages with their own setup, including contract information, price lists, Who's Who, presentations, success stories and a chat room. Team members on existing accounts can continuously update their Global Account Strategic Plan using Docushare.

There is also a Global Account Management Information System that tracks revenue and machine population in 45 countries around the world. Xerox is in the process of upgrading that system and turning it into a Global Account Reporting System. The upgraded system will not only report billed revenue but also track current booked business and an account's gross profit.

Xerox global account operations also has an internal 'best practice' sharing system called Xplane Information Transfer (Xplane i.t.). The idea was developed in Europe and used to share success stories with other global account managers. The Xplane i.t. memos do three things. First, they highlight applications and solutions so that other employees involved in global accounts are aware of them. Second, they give recognition to the people who are responsible for success stories. Third, they provide a constructive piece of news for everybody in the company to say, 'Hey, we've had success here, business is good with this account.'

GLOBAL ACCOUNT PLANNING AND COORDINATION

Xerox uses its global account planning process to balance both global and local issues. If it is adding a new global account, key members who will be handling and interacting with the account come together to develop a coordinated plan during the account planning process. In that process Xerox involves many of the people who will be handling the account, including key members from Xerox's local, corporate and industry groups, as well as representatives from partners who will be involved and sometimes representatives from the account. The account representative is an executive and comes to the account planning meeting to bring the account's perspective into the planning process. If an executive from the account is not able to attend the meeting, the Xerox global account manager will visit the relevant account executive to collect customer information to be taken into consideration during the process. Xerox employees involved in the planning process meeting are the ones who will handle major aspects of the account and related initiatives. A global account plan can be updated throughout the year, if needed, on Docushare.

Independent of the account planning meetings, Xerox schedules an annual global account meeting that combines a kick-off meeting for the up-coming year, recognition of success and training.

Xerox controls the account plan from a global perspective through influence and corporate backing. However, friction sometimes does occur between the needs and objectives of global account management and those of product and local management. For example, there may be cases of maverick managers trying to sell out products at the end of June because they want to make their half-year bonus, or a country manager may sell to the local division of a global account for 10 per cent less than the global contract stipulates just to get the business.

This kind of behaviour is technically out of the control of the global account manager because he or she does not have direct control at the local level. However, this is not a major problem for Xerox because, in general, most managers understand and follow the global account management concepts. A manager is hard pressed to argue a conflicting direction if there is a plan that has been put together by the global account team and the customer has sanctioned it. Issues do not escalate very often at Xerox because the global account management programme has been working for almost 15 years and managers know that 'you shouldn't mess with the global account manager' because people recognize that they have ownership of the account.

SELECTING AND DEVELOPING GLOBAL ACCOUNT MANAGERS

Approximately 50 per cent of Xerox's global account managers have been national account managers. They were usually elevated to the position when an account was elevated from national account status to global account status, but this scenario is not guaranteed. For example, in 2000 Xerox elevated a large server company from a national account in the United States to a global account because of its global expansion. In this case, the person who was the national account manager did not get the job because Xerox industry management did not feel that person was sufficiently capable of taking on the additional responsibility. National account managers and global account managers have similar jobs at Xerox, except for the degree of complexity, difficulty and cultural acumen required. A national account manager with less refined human management skills might perform well in the US because he or she is dealing with other Americans in English and does not have to master other languages or cultural difficulties.

Global account managers often deal with remote people who do not report to them. In these situations, they must manage through influence. They must understand how to communicate with people from another culture. Xerox understands that a key to success is managing customer perceptions of its people and how they deal with all kinds of issues.

Xerox is in the process of working on professional development and focusing on what is required for the global account manager to be successful on a worldwide basis. Working with Rutgers University and the Strategic Account Management Association, Xerox has carried out elaborate skills assessment internally with sales people, middle management, senior management and customers to determine the skills and competencies required to be a successful global account manager. Qualified global account managers are difficult to find and Xerox is constrained by its inability to identify and attract a sufficient number of candidates. Given this situation, approximately a third of Xerox's global account managers are stretched too thin. Xerox has developed some cultural awareness half-day modules for employees involved in global accounts. These modules create awareness and train participants to use a mental checklist that asks, 'What's going on here? Are we having a conflict because we do not treat time the same? Or we do not reason the same way? Or we do not treat status the same way?'

Xerox conducted workshop sessions at the headquarters of Fuji-Xerox Asia Pacific in Singapore, which brought together country-based marketing people and their global account counterparts from the Asia Pacific region and global account managers from around the world. Account managers presented their account plans, made calls on their customers and listened to what other account managers had to say about business in their respective countries. Xerox found that the participants who were experienced and aware of cultural differences provided the greatest value.

Xerox is organized by industry. Five industry business groups develop industry-specific solutions and each is responsible for gathering and analysing its respective industry. The five industry business groups are Graphic Arts, Public Sector, Healthcare, Financial Services and Industrial. Each industry business group is organized into sub-units that focus on specific niches. For example, the Industrial Business Group is organized into sub-units including Aerospace, Automotive and Other Discrete Manufacturing, Petroleum and Chemical, Communications, Consumer Products, Pharmaceutical, Technology, Transportation and Utilities. Each industry sub-unit has marketing managers who track specific industries.

Industry group team members are knowledgeable in their specific industries; about 40 per cent were hired out of those industries. For example, the Public Sector Business Group hired a person who was an executive with the state of Florida to become the university and education marketing manager. He knew the language and culture of the public sector and the education industry. Each industry group marketing manager puts together training sessions and seminars specific to his or her industry. It is also the responsibility of the industry groups to develop solutions for their particular industries. For example, in the pharmaceutical industry the new drug approval process is very complicated and it is the responsibility of the pharmaceutical sub-unit to know the procedure, required paperwork and software solutions.

When it comes to individual global accounts, it is the responsibility of the account manager and the people on the global account team to meet the account's specific informational requirements. Most of this work is done when the annual account plan is drawn up. As previously mentioned, the annual account planning process at Xerox sometimes includes participation from the global account customer. This provides an account team with valuable first-hand information about the account's business problems and critical success factors. In some circumstances where Xerox has had a strong relationship with a global account or there is an adept global account manager on the account, customers have volunteered information by saying, 'By the way, here are a few areas where I think you can help us.'

Xerox's global account managers receive training on industries from the industry managers. The global account management programme office is focused on what is required to be a successful strategic account manager on a global basis. This includes developing a manager's skills in cultural awareness, reading financial reports, executive communication, managing cross-cultural teams without direct authority, major international economic trends and understanding the influences of currency fluctuations on business. Xerox is trying to make global account managers trusted advisers to the customer. It can easily lose credibility if a global account manager and a customer are having a conversation and the customer says, 'We're going to have to postpone that order in Singapore because of what's been happening with the value of the currency' and the global account manager looks at the customer and asks, 'So what difference does that make?' The global account manager should be aware enough to ask, 'How about if we did an offshore deal and you pay for it in the UK?'

GLOBAL ACCOUNT MEASUREMENT SYSTEMS

To determine the success of its global account management programme, Xerox uses both qualitative and quantitative measures. The principal measurement used is year-over-year revenue growth of each global account. Since 2000, Xerox has been measuring the gross profit of its global accounts. This has been difficult because of multiple P&L allocations versus actual costs. It also measures customer satisfaction. Some of the softer measures employed are the degree to which Xerox has been able to introduce new technologies into its global accounts, the conversion rate from analogue to digital and the adoption rate of colour products.

Xerox's global account managers are compensated based on year-over-year revenue growth and profit growth. A global account manager may also be measured on how well he or she is able to get the global account team to use Docushare and work together as a team.

CREATING VALUE FOR GLOBAL ACCOUNTS

A major part of the global account manager's role is to identify unique ways to create value for the account. Xerox has developed most of these solutions from an industry orientation, with most of the advancements coming from global accounts. For example, BMW wanted to make vehicle owner's manuals personalized and less expensive to produce. Most vehicle owner's manuals included at least four languages of material and instructions for all the possible options. The traditional owner's manual was about an inch and a half thick. This practice wasted paper, was becoming more expensive to print and had high associated storage costs. Xerox worked with BMW for almost a year to create a personalized print-on-demand owner's manual solution. With this solution, BMW was able to provide an owner's manual that was personalized, with the buyer's name printed on the front, in the buyer's preferred language and with instructions that addressed only the specific options purchased. The new owner's manuals are 80 per cent thinner than those previously used and are printed on demand, thus eliminating storage and shipping costs. The personalized print-on-demand owner's manual solution has become almost a generic solution now: Xerox is using the format for mobile phone companies, like Nokia and Motorola, and television manufacturing companies.

Xerox has also worked closely with global account pharmaceutical companies. It has software that helps pharmaceutical companies manage the proposals involved in the drug approval process. The drug development and testing process needs to be meticulously documented with version control and sign-off for all the different tests for drug approval. If all the documents required for a drug approval process were printed, they would fill a trailer truck. Xerox has worked with its pharmaceutical global accounts to do this electronically.

Another area where Xerox has been successful is in the banking industry. It has been able to help many banks, with the Hong Kong and Shanghai Bank as a prime example. Xerox worked with Hong Kong and Shanghai Bank to have print-on-demand personalized bank statements. The bank can now actually ask customers 'What language do you want your statement printed in?' and immediately print a personalized version.

GLOBAL ACCOUNT MANAGEMENT CHALLENGES

One of the biggest issues that Xerox faces is the lack of a truly shared value among all senior management as to the importance of the global account management programme and the level of support it requires. Nobody wants to give up control. For example, the German managers do not want to give up control of BMW and so they resist having to go into a corporate function. They also do not want the salesperson from Germany to spend all of his or her time doing business in France, the UK or Italy. This is because Xerox Germany does not receive credit for revenue developed in other countries while incurring the cost of paying the salesperson's salary and traveling expenses. Germany has eight global account managers on its payroll and they are only spending about a third of their time in Germany. That is an unfair burden for the current general manager of Germany. There is also the issue of Xerox Germany losing the services within Germany of the individual account manager while he or she is doing business elsewhere.

Another challenge for Xerox's global account management is to determine how to handle customers who want a global price. Although the customer might want the same prices everywhere, Xerox does not have the same costs everywhere. Many customers do not recognize this, even though they may talk to someone like

McDonald's that does not charge the same price for a 'Big Mac' everywhere, or to automobile companies who do not sell comparable automobiles for the same prices everywhere.

Xerox global account management has not lost too many deals because it could not provide a global price. Xerox has had situations where business has been postponed or lost temporarily when another company was awarded a contract because it claimed that it could provide a global price. However, usually these companies cannot actually provide a global price when it comes to delivery. The global pricing problem tends to be with uninitiated customers: their purchasing people want to try to do this because they want a feather in their cap and say 'We've got the same price everywhere'. Xerox could give customers the same price everywhere if the pricing were smoothed out, but that means some countries would be paying a price higher than they could get locally.

Marriott International: Global Account Management

Marriott International (MI), established in 1927, was a Washington DC-based hospitality company with over 2200 operating units worldwide. In 2000, MI employed 153 000 people in 60 countries and generated $19.8 billion in sales.

OVERVIEW

MI had 20 products divided into six segments: Full Service Lodging, Selected Service Lodging, Extended Stay and Corporate Living, Ownership Resorts, Senior Living and Other Operations. Full Service Lodging consisted of Marriott hotels, resorts and suites, Renaissance hotels, resorts and suites, The Ritz-Carlton Hotel Company, LLC and Marriott Conference Center. Selected Service Lodging consisted of Courtyard, Fairfield Inn, Spring Hill Suites and Armada International. Extended Stay and Corporate Living consisted of Residence Inn TownePlace Suites, Marriott Executive Apartments and ExecuStay. Ownership Resorts consisted of Marriott Vacation Club International, The Ritz-Carlton Club and Horizons by Marriott Vacation Club.

This case was prepared by W. Caleb McCann, MBA, Babson College, under the direction of H. David Hennessey, Associate Professor of Marketing and International Business.

This case was drawn entirely from public information sources and written as a basis for class discussion rather than to illustrate either effective or ineffective handling of a business situation.

Senior Living consisted of Brighton Gardens, Marriott MapleRidge and Village Oaks. Other Operations included Marriott Distribution Services and The Market Place by Marriott.

In 1999 1 per cent of the hotels in the MI system were company owned; the rest were franchised, being owned and financed by third parties. Franchise fees made up 17 per cent of MI's 1999 earnings, base management fees 27 per cent, profit participations 38 per cent, timeshare resorts 15 per cent and land rentals 3 per cent.

INTERNATIONAL EXPANSION

In October 1966, MI expanded internationally by acquiring an airline catering company in Caracas, Venezuela. Between 1967 and 1989 MI acquired restaurant chains, fast-food restaurant chains, airport terminal food services, beverage and merchandise facilities, a vacation timesharing business, two diversified food service companies, a contract food service company, an all-suite hotel chain, a housekeeping maintenance and laundry service and a rental retirement community.

In addition, between 1967 and 1989 MI continued to build its existing hotel and restaurant system, primarily in the United States. In April 1987, it completed the largest single-site reservations operation in the United States. Between 1989 and 1995, it grew from 18 to 60 international (non-US) hotels. In March 1997, MI acquired Renaissance Hotel Group for roughly $1 billion and increased its international presence to 235 hotels.

ORGANIZATIONAL TRANSFORMATION

In June 1996 a CEO-sponsored taskforce set up to analyse the effectiveness of the salesforce led to the development of a customer relationship management (CRM) programme. This in turn led to a sales transformation programme in 1997. This consolidated the sales division, marketing division and customer services function into one reporting structure and business unit, except for the international salesforce. International sales continued to report to international operations.

The organizational transformation included the creation of a Strategic Accounts division within the Sales and Marketing division. This was responsible for MI's global and US-headquartered national accounts. Global and US-headquartered national accounts consisted of approximately 1500 commercial customers and annual sales of roughly $3 billion. The Strategic Accounts division sits above the hotels' salesforces and builds account teams around qualified commercial customers. In the course of the transformation, MI also consolidated Marriott.com, worldwide reservations, agency sales and field sales under the Sales and Marketing division.

Before MI had instituted the transformation process and new account management strategy, individual hotels acting alone to create demand handled their own sales and marketing. There was a system-wide salesforce of 225 000 who sold for individual properties.

STRATEGIC SELLING THROUGH ACCOUNT MANAGEMENT

The Strategic Accounts division created the MI Alliance Programme. This was initiated when senior managers realized that major customers, primarily corporations, were demanding more than just hotel rooms: they wanted accommodation solutions. A decision to reorganize the entire salesforce within the company was based on three goals: using technology to support connectivity; refocusing the salesforce on markets rather than individual hotels; and developing a global account management programme.

In 1998 MI created a Global Account Management (GAM) group. It hired a GAM team of 12 global account managers. These managers were chosen after review of candidates' detailed resumés, psychological profile testing and interviews by two vice-presidents. A committee of five vice-presidents from brand teams, corporate headquarters and sales and marketing approved GAM directors.

There were four levels of account management. Tier IV accounts consisted of several thousand local accounts and new prospects. Tier

III consisted of several hundred regional accounts. Tier II consisted of a few hundred national accounts. Tier I, Alliance Accounts, consisted of global business customers. Out of 3500 total accounts, the GAM group identified 25–50 potential Alliance Accounts, MI's label for highly valued global customers. In 1998, MI's 30 Alliance Accounts accounted for $600 million in revenues and were managed by 12 global account managers.

By 1999, MI's salesforce was completely overhauled and organized around customers instead of around properties. In 1999 MI employed over 10 000 sales and reservation associates, all of whom carried out booking requests for any MI property worldwide.

INTERNAL SELLING

For the alliance programme to begin properly, MI had to sell the idea internally. It faced the challenge of moving the salesforce from a traditional transactional structure to an organization focused on account solutions. Since each hotel in the MI system was franchised and managed locally and each had a separate P&L statement, consolidation of account management initially was seen as a loss of control by individual hotel management. To address this issue, MI conducted an internal campaign focused on selling the account strategy programme. Communication of the vision, mission and plan was continuous. For every presentation that was given to an external customer selling the account management strategy, three presentations were given to those involved internally.

The GAM programme was mainly concerned with meeting the needs of strategic accounts and not with filling rooms at individual hotels. During account management formation and the early stages of execution, MI continually communicated the urgency for change and every success was celebrated and communicated to all involved. This was achieved through e-mail by relaying real success stories praising work that encouraged and advanced strategic selling. MI brought in customers and conducted one-to-one presentations to help transform the sales team. Quarterly updates were given during business reviews. During the first year alone, the vice-president of alliance sales held over 80 internal meetings addressing alliance accounts. Sales training classes for 500 plus people were held every year specifically to demonstrate how strategic account management would change each job in the company.

MI's alliance programme identified audiences throughout the company who were critical to its success. These groups were targeted with constant communications for the purpose of providing information that helped them understand the programme's strategy and gain their support. Alliance programme directors and vice-presidents were on the agenda of every corporate meeting throughout the organization. Sales newsletters, in-market presentations, monthly conference calls with each account team and annual business review meetings with executives were some of the other internal communication media used to get the message across. Many of these initiatives continued even after the programme had advanced beyond its start-up period.

Compensation packages for sales teams also changed, moving from calculating sales on 'definite room nights' to 'total account revenue'. The weighting of the revenue component decreased from 80 to 50 per cent, annual account revenue goals were zero based and account team members had a portion of their compensation plans tied to supporting strategic accounts.

GLOBAL ACCOUNT MANAGEMENT

Tier I Alliance Account was MI's category for global accounts. The GAM strategy was business-to-business focused; that is, the programme concentrated on providing a greater level of service to companies that used MI on a regular basis. This was done by profiling and segmenting potential accounts to ensure alignment with the programme. Then a GAM team assigned to key customers would identify its influencers, determine its requirements and needs and develop a customized value proposal for the customer.

MI's goal was to get customers who could be potential alliance accounts to think beyond price and a single point of contact. At first, many customers saw the MI GAM programme as only a central point of contact and global pricing agreement. This was important for MI's strategy but only the beginning step. Its long-term vision was to combine its strengths with that of an alliance account and leverage this relationship to generate solutions and create value for both companies. Building a relationship of trust and satisfying a customer's base expectations was MI's first step in this process. Its approach was flawlessly to execute an alliance account's initial expectations regarding one point of contact and pricing. Through delivering small successes, MI believed that a relationship of trust would grow and open up the customer to complete acceptance of the alliance account strategy.

MI's long-term GAM strategy success is illustrated by its relationship with International Business Machines (IBM). MI appointed a global account manager to manage the IBM account and direct a sales team of about 70 to manage the local relationships. A year after MI designated IBM as an alliance account, IBM agreed to use MI as its only supplier when piloting new accommodation, conferences and other related event programmes. In 1998 IBM paid MI over $2 million in cancellation fees for meeting rooms. In that same year, it paid MI $15 million for meeting rooms actually used. Thus, it was paying over 10 per cent of its budget for meetings on cancellation fees. Through the alliance account partnership IBM and MI had built, the two companies worked together to solve this problem. The solution involved connecting MI and IBM's internal systems with an electronic bulletin board on which IBM would post cancelled meeting rooms to sell to other internal IBM customers. If another IBM customer filled the meeting room, then the cancellation fee would no longer apply. This way IBM dramatically reduced money spent on cancellation fees and MI did not have to assume the costs of filling a previously scheduled meeting room.

TECHNOLOGY

MI aligned its IT organization to reflect the transformation of its sales and marketing functions. This included providing every business and functional division in MI with a representative from the IT division, consolidating databases, enhancing data-warehousing capabilities and developing customer-profiling capabilities. The IT representatives reported directly to their appointed business or functional division. The Strategic Accounts division had its own IT representative.

MI invested approximately $25 million in a Siebel front-office system. It had about 2500 employees using the system in 2000 and planned to have between 4000 and 5000 employees implemented by the end of 2001. During the Siebel front-office system rollout, MI intended to consolidate many of its various customer information databases to improve its storage and use of customer information.

MI kept customer profiles by collecting and storing transaction history, demographics, product and service usage, customer value level and service history. It systematically recorded data at each interaction with customers and was able to view a complete customer profile across all product and service areas by downloading data from multiple databases. Data warehousing was completely functioning in the consumer business, which enabled the operation of MI's loyalty programme and reservation for the individual traveller. This was not the case with business customers because the inventory management (meeting rooms and conference sites) was controlled at the property site level. Business customer information and bookings needed to be uploaded to be directly accessed company wide. The database consolidation and the Siebel system allowed for business customers' and individual customers' information to be accessible company-wide. In 2001 MI began to develop a total hotel yield management and consolidated inventory system for meeting and conference rooms and meeting space.

Through its website, MI provided customers with the ability to browse for hotel rooms, make reservations, link to other travel sites and create customer profiles. In 2001, it expected to book $1 billion in business through its website. The Strategic Accounts division planned and conducted pilot programmes to develop MI's web presence for business customers. These programmes included links to unique sites of interest to business travellers and provided online booking capability for meeting planners by linking into companies' intranets.

Hewlett-Packard Company: Global Account Management

Hewlett-Packard Company (HP), established in 1939, was a Palo Alto, California-based technology company with more than 540 sales and support offices worldwide. In 2000, HP employed 88 500 people in 120 countries and generated $48 billion in revenues.

HP's first product was an electronic instrument used to test sound equipment. In 1957 its written objectives along with its management style formed the 'HP Way'. Dave Packard delivered the corporate objectives as a way of guiding management decision making. In 1958 divisions structured with separate profit-and-loss accountability were established. Each product group was a self-sustaining organization responsible for developing, manufacturing and marketing its own products. Any group that grew to 1500 people was divided in two and moved to two separate P&Ls. This autonomy fostered individual motivation, initiative and creativity, and gave employees the opportunity to work with broad freedom to achieve common goals and objectives.

In 1959 HP became global and opened a large manufacturing facility in Boeblingen, Germany and a European headquarters in Geneva, Switzerland. Flexible work hours were introduced at the Boeblingen plant in 1967 and throughout US facilities in 1973. In 1968,

This case was prepared by W. Caleb McCann, MBA, Babson College, under the direction of H. David Hennessey, Associate Professor of Marketing and International Business.

The case was drawn entirely from public information sources and written as a basis for class discussion rather than to illustrate either effective or ineffective handling of a business situation.

Copyright © 2001 by Babson College, William F. Glavin Center for Global Entrepreneurial Leadership. Not to be used or reproduced without written permission.

decentralization moved decision making from corporate vice-presidents to group general managers who ran divisions with related product lines. This allowed compatible units to work together.

HP's first step in adopting a group structure was combining independent operating divisions to form related product groups. It was again reorganized in 1984 into a four-sector organization that was formed to oversee the growing number of groups. From 1986–1987 all of HP's technical computing activities were put into the same sector. In 1994 telecommuting policies were formalized, making HP one of the first companies to encourage telecommuting around the world. Employees could work at home or at remote HP offices. HP benefited from reduced office-space requirements and improved employee retention. Its intranet, the world's largest at the time, linked its global operations and ensured communication with employees wherever located.

EXTENDED ENTERPRISE

In response to continuous rising expectations and competition, HP introduced technology initiatives to increase speed, reduce costs and improve quality. These initiatives worked through the Internet both internally and externally, with customers and with suppliers. In 1989, HP implemented its global wide-area network, which has resulted in cost savings of five times the previous system. In 1999, 1.5 million e-mail messages were transmitted daily and the number of megabytes of traffic continued to grow, with the increasing number of attachments.

HP used its intranet to increase sales productivity with the aid of its new tool called Electronic Sales Partner (ESP). This tool anticipated the informational needs of HP's sales representatives. It had increased sales productivity and saved HP $125 million per year. It gave salespeople access to any information they need to do their job, including field training, product literature, press releases, data sheets and conference guides, all in one place whenever they needed it. ESP's primary users were 5000 sales representatives. In 1999, ESP contained over 40 000 documents and was continuing to grow.

One of the first functions where HP began to extend information out to its trading partners was in order fulfilment and logistics. Its web-based product data management had links with material resource planning (MRP) and corporate parts databases. Its workflow engine controls changes, approvals, versions, notification and summary statistics. The channel logistics and fulfilment organization distributes HP products to about 250 resellers in the US and Canada, and it pushes $20 billion of product through the reseller channel annually.

GLOBAL ACCOUNT MANAGEMENT

Marketing within the computer systems industry evolved towards a customer-focused approach in the late 1980s and early 1990s for several reasons. First, customers demanded consistent worldwide service and support and increased standardization. Second, technologies changed from a centralized mainframe mode to decentralized networked computers that were linked globally. Multinational customers demanded that vendors be strategic partners who could demonstrate an understanding of specific international business needs and deploy relevant solutions on a global basis. Third, continuous innovation and decreasing time to market forced firms to reevaluate their relationships and strategic alliances with customers and suppliers. Fourth, alternative channels of distribution were prevalent and continued to grow throughout the industry.

In 1991, HP implemented a pilot global account management programme between its largest division, the Computer Systems Organization, and six of its global accounts. This programme originated from the philosophy of customer-based management. HP's global account management programme consisted of several elements:

- *Global client business managers* were assigned executives and account programme managers. This level of global account management, offering one interface to account executives, greatly facilitated communications for global account customers.

- *Experts and specialists* on product solutions.
- The process of *worldwide contracts*, delivery and implementation, primarily through HP's intranet.

In response to customers' expectations for all parts of HP to behave as one company, HP consolidated its sales model by creating the 'client business manager' in 1998. This position was responsible for complete business relationships of customers in HP's Computer Organization. This created some challenges, because organization structures below the client business manager were not changed or aligned.

GLOBAL ACCOUNT MANAGERS

Global account managers were directed to address customers' demands for consistent worldwide service. Global account managers were located near customers' headquarters, were responsible for directly managing HP's relationship with the global customer, and served as the direct channel of the global account's relationship to HP's distribution channels. The global account manager's responsibilities included coordination of global customer sales, providing customer support and satisfaction, ensuring that HP was seen as one company at all customer locations, working with HP's senior management to ensure that company actions were organized and availability of adequate resources to service global account opportunities properly, and establishing close relationships with senior corporate HP executives assigned to the global accounts.

Global account managers operated under a dual reporting system. They reported to the country/region and industry manager as well as to the global account sales manager accountable for global accounts business in a particular field office. The global accounts sales manager reported to both the field operations manager and to the head of the global account programme. Global account headquarters staff reported directly to the global account manager for their field. District sales managers and sales representatives reported both to a global account manager and to a local area sales manager. Dual reporting structures strengthened the geographic responsibilities of the salesforce and enabled the global account manager to meet a global customer's needs directly, making decisions independently of geography.

Global account managers were evaluated on the worldwide performance of their assigned global accounts. Country managers were evaluated on the worldwide performance of global accounts headquartered in their country as well as overall country performance.

HP's global account management programme used a measurement system that was to understand the costs of implementing the programme and provided global account performance tracking. Two metrics were involved in the measurement systems: selling cost envelope (SCE) and the account specific field selling cost model (FSC). SCE measured the selling costs associated with obtaining an order and FSC measured all costs associated with the implementation of a global account sales team and supporting costs.

Global account managers are responsible for motivating the local sales teams and country-level business managers. In some cases, the business generated by global accounts is 30–40 per cent of a global account manager's business. The global account manager's responsibility to iron out the differences between local needs and global business needs is achieved through meeting, in person, with local salespeople and management.

Bibliography

Abell, Derek F. & Hammond, John S. (1979) *Strategic Market Planning: Problems and Analytical Approaches*, Englewood Cliffs, NJ: Prentice Hall.

Alahuhta, Matti (1990) 'Global growth strategies for high technology challengers', *Acta Polytechnica Scandinavia*, Electrical Engineering Series No. 66, Espoo: Helsinki Technical University.

Allen, Stephen (1990) 'Note on the European Major Home Appliance Industry – 1990' (European Case Clearing House No. 393-091-5), 'Whirlpool Corporation' (European Case Clearing House No. 393-095-1), 'Electrolux' (European Case Clearing House No. 393-094-1), 'General Electric: Major Appliances' (European Case Clearing House No. 393-093-1).

Allen, Stephen (1992) 'Note on the Construction Machinery Industry' (European Case Clearing House No. 393-068-5), 'Caterpillar and Komatsu in 1988' (European Case Clearing House No. 393-069-1), 'Caterpillar and Komatsu in 1992' (European Case Clearing House No. 393-070-1).

Arnold, David & Arnold, Martin (2001) 'Organizing knowledge exchange in global account management', *Strategic Account Management Association Research Series*, pp. 1–39.

Arnold, Martin, Belz, Christian & Senn, Christoph (2001) 'Leveraging knowledge in global key account management', *Thexis*, 1st quarter, pp. 1–74.

Belz, Christian, Müllner, Markus & Zupancic, Dirk (2001) 'Performers and organizational structures in international key account management', *Institute of Marketing and Retailing*, February, pp. 1–13.

Blessington, Mark & Sands, Scott (2002) 'Global sales compensation', *Velocity*, Quarter 3.

Bowerin, David (2000) 'Serving global customers globally, delivering the global promise locally: Citibank global relationship banking', *Strategic Account Management Association Annual Conference*, May, pp. 1–23.

Brimson, James A. (1991) *Activity Accounting: An Activity-Based Costing Approach*, Chichester: Wiley.

Business International (1986) 'White goods empire: 400 villages crown Electrolux market king', *Business International*, August 11, p. 250.

BusinessWeek (1987) 'On the verge of a world war in white goods', *BusinessWeek*, November 2, p. 41.

Class, Selena (2002) 'Pharma overview', *Chemical and Engineering News*, December 2, pp. 39–49.

Croom, Simon, Wilson, Kevin, Millman, Tony, Senn, Christoph & Weilbaker, Dan (1999) 'How to meet the challenge of managing global customers', *Velocity*, Fall, pp. 33–45.

Deavenport, Earnest (1999) 'The formula for global account management success', *Velocity*, Summer, pp. 14–17.

Diageo (2003) 'Our history', www.diageo.com/ad/company/our_history.

Donnelly, John (2002) 'Slow growth hurting global poverty fight, World Bank says', *Knight Ridder Tribune Business News*, December 12, p. 1.

Financial Times (1993) 'The world automotive suppliers', *Financial Times*, June 28, Survey, sec. IV.

Financial Times (1998) 'Zurich sets out terms of £23 billion deal with BAT', *Financial Times*, October 17, p. 21.

Fleming, Sandy (1999) 'Global procurement: A universal trend and how Canon succeeds', *Thexis*, 4th quarter, p. 43.

Fortune (1993) 'Capturing the global consumer', *Fortune*, December 13, p. 166.

Fritschi, Anton (1999) 'Global key account management bei ABB: Erfolg kennt keine (Länder-) Grenzen', *Thexis*, Vol. 4, 26–9.

Gadnis, Ashish (1999) 'Is your customer lost in your CRM application?', *Velocity*, Fall, pp. 31–43.

Gartner Group (2001) 'CRM case study: Marriott's B-to-B division achieves relationship manager in Cap Gemini Ernst & Young's CRM Index benchmarking study', Stamford, CT: Gartner Group.

Gilbert, Xavier & Strebel, Paul (1989) 'Taking advantage of industry shifts', *European Management Journal*, Vol. 7, No. 4, pp. 398–402.

Gilbert, Xavier & Strebel, Paul (1991) 'Developing competitive advantage', in Henry Mitzberg & James Brian Quinn, *The Strategy Process*, Prenctice Hall, 2nd edn, pp. 82–93.

Hall, E. T. (1976) *Beyond Culture*, Garden City, NY: Doubleday.

Helsing, Jane (1999) 'Getting internal support for your strategic account management program', *Velocity*, Summer, pp. 6–7, 48.

Hennessey, H. David (2002) 'Discovering the hidden value in global account management', working paper, Wellesley, MA: Babson College.

Hilti, Robert (2001) 'The Hilti Group', *Strategic Account Management Association Annual Meeting*, pp. 1–20.

Hofstede, Geert (1991) *Cultures and Organizations*, London: McGraw-Hill.

Jeannet, Jean-Pierre (1986) 'Jan-Erik Dyvi Shipowners (A) & (B)', case, Lausanne: IMD.

Jeannet, Jean-Pierre (1993a) 'The world paint industry', industry note, Lausanne: IMD.

Jeannet, Jean-Pierre (1993b) 'ICI Paints (A) and (B)', cases, Lausanne: IMD.

Jeannet, Jean-Pierre (1993c) 'Siemens AT: Brazil strategy', case, Lausanne: IMD.

Jeannet, Jean-Pierre (1996a) 'Understanding your industry', note/working paper, Wellesley, MA: Babson College.

Jeannet, Jean-Pierre (1996b) 'Groupe Schneider', case, Wellesley, MA: Babson College.

Jeannet, Jean-Pierre (2000) *Managing with a Global Mindset*, London: Financial Times/Prentice Hall/Pearson.

Jeannet, Jean-Pierre & Hennessey, H. David (2001) *Global Marketing Strategies*, 5th edn, Boston, MA: Houghton Mifflin.

Jenni, Christopher, Senn, Christoph & Zeier, Rene (2002) 'Selling the GAM program internally: The Sika Industry case', *Strategic Account Management Association Annual Conference*, pp. 1–43.

Kerestes, Thomas (1998) 'Praxair: The anatomy of successful global customer management program', *National Account Management Association 34th Annual Conference*, pp. 1–29.

Kieschke, Joy (2001) 'Lucent Technologies global account management program', *Strategic Account Management Association Annual Conference*, May, pp. 1–30.

Kotler, Philip (2002) *Marketing Management: Analysis, Planning, Implementation, and Control*, 11th edn, Englewood Cliffs, NJ: Prentice Hall.

Kotler, Philip & Armstrong, Gary (2000) *Principles of Marketing*, 9th edn, Englewood Cliffs, NJ: Prentice-Hall.

LaNasa, Julie M. (2002) 'Solectron: Building customer teams to deliver on your company's value proposition', *Velocity*, Quarter 1, pp. 33–36.

Lanning, Michael (1998) *Delivering Profitable Value*, Reading, MA: Perseus Books, p. 41.

Levitt, Theodore (1983) 'The globalization of markets', *Harvard Business Review*, May/June, pp. 92–102.

Lorenz, Christopher (1989) 'The birth of a transnational', *McKinsey Quarterly*, Autumn, p. 72.

Macaulay, David (2001) 'Siemens informational communications: Corporate account management', *Strategic Account Management Association Annual Conference*, pp. 1–12.

McCann, Caleb (2001a) 'Interview of Nikos Liapis of Steelcase', September 6.

McCann, Caleb (2001b) 'Interview of office products company', September 6.

McCann, Caleb (2001c) 'Interview of Danny Van der Sande, VP European Trade Management at Henkel Group', November 5.

McCann, Caleb (2001d) 'Interview of Ron Moore, Global Accounts Manager at Fritz', November 28.

McCann, Caleb & Hennessey, H. David (2002a) 'Critical factors in global account management', working paper, Wellesley, MA: Babson College.

McCann, Caleb & Hennessey, H. David (2002b) 'Marriott International: Global account management program', case, Wellesley, MA: Babson College.

Medical Advertising News (2002) 'R&D costs are staggering', *Medical Advertising News*, February, Vol. 21, No. 2, p. 1.

Millman, Tony & Wilson, Kevin (2001) 'Structuring and positioning global account management programmes: A typology', *Journal of Selling and Major Account Management*, Autumn, pp. 11–38.

Montgomery, David & Yip, George (2000) 'The challenge of global customer management', *Marketing Management*, Winter, pp. 22–30.

Montgomery, David, Yip, George & Villalonga, Belen (1999) 'Demand for and use of global account management', Report 99-115, Cambridge, MA: Marketing Science Institute, pp. 1–31.

NAMA (1997) 'NAM/GAM Benchmark Consortium: National account benchmarking', Chicago, IL: National Account Management Association and HR Chally Group Consortium, October.

NAMA (1998) '1998 Strategic Account Management Innovation Study: Oracle Corporation', Chicago, IL: National Account Management Association.

Napolitano, Lisa (1999) 'The state of SAM in Europe', *Velocity*, Spring, pp. 9–11.

Narayandas, Das, Quelch, John & Swartz, Gordon (2000) 'Prepare your company for global pricing', *Sloan Management Review*, Fall, pp. 61–70.

Parr, Jay (2001) 'Cisco's strategic accounts program', *Strategic Account Management Association Annual Conference*, pp. 1–23.

Pope, Atlee & Brown, George (2002) 'Avoiding the vicious cycle of pricing', *Velocity*, Quarter 4, pp. 47–50.

Porter, Michael E. (1980) *Competitive Strategy: Techniques for Analyzing Industries and Competitors*, Boston, MA: Free Press.

Porter, Michael E. (1985) *Competitive Advantage: Creating and Sustaining Superior Performance*, Boston, MA: Free Press.

Richard, Steve & Wilson, Kevin (2000) 'Developing organisational commitment to global strategic account management programmes: The Marriott experience', *Journal of Selling and Major Account Management*, Summer, pp. 66–76.

Ronchez, Ron (1999) 'Modular architecture in the marketing process', *Journal of Marketing*, Vol. 63, pp. 92–111.

SAMA (1999) 'How Dun and Bradstreet Global implemented lessons learned from a world class benchmarking consortium', *Velocity*, Fall, pp. 15–19.

SAMA (2001) 'S4 Consulting Armstrong/Citibank account performance', Chicago, IL: Strategic Account Management Association.

SAMA (2002) 'Marriott International SAMA Performance Award', Chicago, IL: Strategic Account Management Association.

Samuelson, Paul A. & Nordhaus, William D. (1989) *Economics*, 13th edn, New York, NY: McGraw-Hill.

Scholl, Stefan (2001) 'International customer management at P&G', Brussels: A.T. Kearney, pp. 1–17. Presented at the SAMA European Forum, October 24, 2001.

Scott, Elliot & Ingalls, Gidgett (2001) 'Leading edge compensation design for strategic account management programs', *Strategic Account Management Association Annual Conference*, May, pp. 1–56.

Senn, Chistoph (1999) 'Implementing global account management: A process oriented approach', *Journal of Selling and Major Account Management*, Vol. 1, No. 3, February, pp. 10–19.

Sperry, Joseph P. (2000) 'Giant companies, small details: 3M and IBM co-creating value at all levels', *Velocity*, Quarter 3, pp. 16–17.

Strebel, Paul (1992) *Breakpoints: How Managers Exploit Radical Business Change*, Boston, MA: Harvard Business School Press.

Uittendroek, Robin (2000) 'Global account management at IBM', *SAMA Annual Meeting*, pp. 1–30.

United Nations (1993) *World Competitiveness Report 1993*, New York, NY: United Nations Conference on Trade and Development.

Wall Street Journal (1998) 'Consolidation in auto-parts industry globally has shifted into high gear', *Wall Street Journal*, February 20, p. B98.

Weilbaker, Dan (1999) 'Compensation issues for global account management', *Journal of Selling and Major Account Management*, Autumn, pp. 88–95.

Weinstein, David (1998) 'Van Leer Packaging Worldwide: The TOTAL Account, Cases A-E', Fontainebleau: INSEAD.

Williams, Geoffrey G. (2001) 'Schneider Electric/Square D', *Strategic Account Management Association Annual Conference*, May, pp. 1–30.

Wilson, Kevin (1999a) *Managing Customer Relationships: A Guide for Strategic Accounts*, www.questteam.com.

Wilson, Kevin (1999b) 'Developing global account management programmes: Observations from a GAM panel presentation', *Thexis*, 4th quarter, pp. 30–35.

Wilson, Kevin (2001) 'The political entrepreneur: Are we seeing a new management role emerging with the global account?', *Focus: Europe*, 1st quarter, pp. 7–11.

Wilson, Kevin, Croom, Simon, Millman, Tony & Weilbaker, Dan (2000) *The Global Account Management Study Research Report*, Sales Research Trust, pp. 1–24.

Yip, George & Madsen, Tammy (1996) 'Global account management: The new frontier in relationship marketing', *International Marketing Review*, Vol. 13, No. 3, pp. 24–42.

Yoshino, Michael & Jeannet, Jean-Pierre (1995) 'Case: Ares-Serono', Boston, MA: Harvard Business School.

Index